Creating Equitable Practices in PBIS

This go-to resource guides educators on how to incorporate equitable practices in a PBIS framework. The authors cover core concepts including school-wide positive behavioral interventions and supports (SWPBIS) and multi-tiered system of supports (MTSS), define equity, and present methods for enhancing implementation practices through an equity mindset. Chapters also include an analysis of team structures and the evaluation of baseline data sources, walking readers through how to incorporate effective practices to support an integrated MTSS framework and produce sustainable outcomes. This book is ideal for educators, behavioral specialists, and administrators who wish to promote a positive school climate and purposeful educational relationships.

Nikole Y. Hollins-Sims is an educational consultant and former Special Assistant to the Secretary of Education for the Pennsylvania Department of Education, and the 2021 Pennsylvania School Psychologist of the Year.

Erica J. Kaurudar is an educational consultant at the Pennsylvania Training and Technical Assistance Network (PaTTAN), where she serves as the Statewide Lead for the School Psychology initiative.

Timothy J. Runge is a nationally certified school psychologist and board certified behavior analyst. He is Professor in the Department of Psychology at Indiana University of Pennsylvania.

T0384866

Creating Equitable Practices in PBIS

Growing a Positive School Climate
for Sustainable Outcomes

Nikole Y. Hollins-Sims, Erica J. Kaurudar, and
Timothy J. Runge

Routledge
Taylor & Francis Group

NEW YORK AND LONDON

Designed cover image: © Getty Images

First published 2023
by Routledge
605 Third Avenue, New York, NY 10158

and by Routledge
4 Park Square, Milton Park, Abingdon, Oxon, OX14 4RN

Routledge is an imprint of the Taylor & Francis Group, an informa business

Library of Congress Cataloging-in-Publication Data
Names: Hollins-Sims, Nikole Y., author. | Kaurudar, Erica J., author. |
    Runge, Timothy J., author.
Title: Creating equitable practices in PBIS : growing a positive school
    climate for sustainable outcomes / Nikole Y. Hollins-Sims, Erica J.
    Kaurudar, Timothy J. Runge.
Other titles: Creating equitable practices in positive behavioral
    interventions and support
Description: New York, NY : Routledge, 2023. | Includes bibliographical
    references.
Identifiers: LCCN 2022030060 (print) | LCCN 2022030061 (ebook) |
Subjects: LCSH: Learning disabled children—Education. | Multi-tiered
    systems of support (Education) | Behavior modification. | School
    improvement programs. | Classroom management. | Educational
    equalization.
Classification: LCC LC4705 .H63 2023 (print) | LCC LC4705 (ebook) |
    DDC 371.39/3--dc23/eng/20220707
LC record available at https://lccn.loc.gov/2022030060
LC ebook record available at https://lccn.loc.gov/2022030061

ISBN: 978-1-032-27844-5 (hbk)
ISBN: 978-1-032-26722-7 (pbk)
ISBN: 978-1-003-29435-1 (ebk)

DOI: 10.4324/9781003294351

Typeset in Palatino
by Apex CoVantage, LLC

To my mother, Yvonne Hollins, I owe you everything. You have been my educational blueprint. This book is dedicated to you. I also dedicate this book to my love, Ronald C. Sims, who has been my backbone, my helpmate and my biggest supporter. Lastly, I dedicate this book to my dream, Ronald C. Sims, Jr., who has been my biggest inspiration and my heartbeat each and every day. Finally, I wish to honor and remember my father, Mr. John Hollins. I hope you are proud of your "pookie".

— Nikole Y. Hollins-Sims

In memory of my grandmother, Betty.

— Erica J. Kaurudar

To all the educators, administrators, families, and students who taught me so much about how schools support the development of future generations— thank you. It is my hope that this book finds a receptive audience and plays a role in improving how schools support the needs of all students. I dedicate this work to my wife, Jean, and daughters, Julia, Sophie, and Emma; your support and love is immeasurable. For that, I am truly blessed.

— Timothy J. Runge

Contents

1

Setting the Foundation

Introduction

Positive behavioral interventions and supports (PBIS) is a preventative framework designed to promote positive school climate, clear expectations, and purposeful educational relationships. Events, including the COVID-19 pandemic and the national climate around social justice, impacted educational systems in an unprecedented way. Equity, inclusion, and belonging (EIB) in education became increasingly relevant to the educational landscape in the midst of those societal shifts. Although equity has been a necessary consideration for service delivery in schools, educational *inequities* have often been the norm rather than the exception.

Throughout the remainder of this text, we will use a variety of terms. We recognize that there are many overlaps in vocabulary connected to school improvement frameworks. The umbrella term that describes the framework comprising academic, behavior, and social-emotional competencies is often referred to as a multi-tiered system of supports (MTSS). The Center on Multi-Tiered System of Supports defines MTSS as "a proactive and preventative framework that integrates data and instruction to maximize student achievement

DOI: 10.4324/9781003294351-1

and support students social, emotional, and behavior needs from a strengths-based perspective" (Essential Components of MTSS, n.d., para. 1). Additionally, response to intervention (RTI) is another term, often used alongside MTSS. RTI is typically defined as the "methodology that is used to determine how slow is slow (rate of growth) and how low is low (student's level of performance), as an alternative to ability-achievement discrepancy within a comprehensive Specific Learning Disability (SLD) Determination process" (Pennsylvania Training and Technical Assistance Network, 2018, para. 1). While each of these terms are important and support key domains of academic, behavior, and social-emotional competencies, we will be using the term PBIS throughout this book. This provides an intentional focus on creating an equitable PBIS framework to foundationally support the future work integration teams may pursue to enhance equitable practices across domains.

This book was developed to evaluate how equity is achieved in schools, leveraging frameworks such as PBIS, with an intended audience of core MTSS/PBIS teams. With any new approach or concept, it is important for readers to begin with a foundational overview of core concepts, including definitions of key terms, such as MTSS, PBIS, and equity. While definitions are important for universal understanding, the application of these concepts through implementation science allows for school-based teams to consider the contextual approaches that will best support all students. These teams will need to consider historical and current opportunities, access, and outcomes which suggest the need for a systemic approach to reduce disproportionality. Research has supported the use of a tiered framework for behavior to improve school climate and reduce problem behaviors. Although this is encouraging, there still remain students of varying backgrounds who are not benefiting from the standard implementation of a tiered framework (Heidelberg et al., 2022). Equitable tiered frameworks allow for all students to have access and opportunity to educational spaces that support their development and sustain a positive school climate and culture. This chapter seeks to serve as a foundational review of the tiered systems and the relevance of historical and current outcomes driving this important work.

Key Components of Tiered Systems

Kincaid et al., (2016) noted that Positive Behavior Supports (PBS) is an umbrella term used to identify a host of approaches that focus on changing social behavior within any ecology. PBS that is implemented within school-age (PreK–12th grade) settings is commonly known as school-wide positive behavioral interventions and supports (SWPBIS). Implementation of PBS within preschool settings is commonly referred to as program-wide positive behavioral interventions and supports (PW-PBIS). While we address equity within a SWPBIS structure in this text, many of these principles and practices likely have application within PW-PBIS.

Positive Behavioral Intervention and Supports (PBIS) is not a curriculum but a multi-tiered framework for organizing assessments, resources, interventions, and supports for all students in an efficient and effective manner. The result is that schools have an increased capacity to prevent problem behavior from occurring, intentionally reinforce prosocial behavior, develop early warning systems to identify when patterns of problematic behavior are emerging, and quickly deploy resources to address those patterns (Sugai & Horner, 2014). While the number of tiers of support embedded within PBIS varies depending on the model implemented within a school, the most omnipresent PBIS model has three tiers.

Sugai and Horner (2009) offered one of the most comprehensive reviews of the three-tiered PBIS framework. Tier 1 (i.e., primary prevention) includes the assessments, instructional practices, data-based decisions regarding core curriculum, and policies and practices provided to all students. The intent of tier 1 PBIS is to prevent or minimize barriers to learning while concurrently promoting inclusive educational opportunities for all students. More specifically, tier 1 PBIS includes: (1) a majority of staff embracing a positive approach to managing students' behavior, (2) students and staff developing culturally responsive and locally relevant school-wide behavioral expectations, (3) explicit instruction and practicing of school-wide expectations in the natural environments, (4) systematically reinforcing behaviors consistent with the expectations via a token economy, (5) adults providing corrective feedback when students fail to follow the behavioral expectations, (6) triannual screening of students' social, emotional, and behavioral health, (7) utilizing multiple data sources to assess implementation and efficacy, and (8) judiciously using a continuum of punishment procedures for inappropriate behavior. Tier 1 PBIS is provided to all students in a school, although these preventive and low intensity instructional supports are generally effective for about 80%–90% of all students (Gottfredson & Gottfredson, 1996; Runge et al., 2021; Walker et al., 2005).

Advanced tiers of PBIS (i.e., tier 2 and tier 3) are vital to the success of the remaining 10%–20% of students for whom tier 1 PBIS is necessary, but insufficient, to adequately address their needs. Tier 2 PBIS (i.e., secondary prevention) is characterized by consistency between the tier 1 school-wide expectations and tier 2 assessments, instruction, and interventions. Typically this is manifested in small group evidence-based interventions, more frequent observation of student behavior (e.g., weekly) on those school-wide expectations, more frequent communication of students' progress to teachers and families, and a wider array of reinforcers for exhibition of prosocial behaviors (Sugai & Horner, 2009). Despite tier 2 PBIS support being provided to 10%–20% of students, not all students experience success with this intensity of supports (Runge et al., 2021). Hence, tier 3 PBIS is needed for those students who, despite exposure to tiers 1 and 2 PBIS supports, continue to face social, emotional, and/or behavioral difficulties.

Tier 3 PBIS is reserved for the students with the most intense social, emotional, and behavioral needs. Generally speaking, this level of support is needed for 3%–5% of students, with those percentages being slightly higher in the secondary grades (Runge et al., 2021; Sugai & Horner, 2009). Eber and colleagues (2011) described tier 3 PBIS as student-centered and family-oriented services. Consequently, tier 3 supports are characterized by assessments, interventions, supports, and data specific to the needs of the student and their family. Such supports and interventions are resource-intensive; hence, they are utilized only when tiers 1 and 2 PBIS have been implemented with fidelity but have not produced the positive outcomes desired for students.

It is important to note that the comprehensive, three-tiered PBIS model provides the organizational framework, including assessment, data collection and analysis, and resource deployment structures to then embed culturally relevant, evidence-based interventions that meet the needs of students in the school. This is especially the case at the advanced tiers where the continuum and range of interventions will vary from one school to the next. As a result, no two schools will offer the same menu of supplemental supports at the advanced tiers. By way of example, an elementary school within which one of the authors consulted had a modest number of students whose parent(s) were incarcerated for drug violations. Consequently, a psychoeducational counseling group was created and facilitated by the school counselor as a means to provide supplemental support to these students. Obviously this was an advanced tier support that was unique to this school. In another school, a tier 2 group was formed around hunting and gun safety given the prevalence rate of middle school students who hunted. Again, a culturally relevant supplemental support is one that fits the unique needs of the school and local community.

Nearly three decades of research have established PBIS as an effective framework for supporting students' needs across a number of important outcomes. Initial empirical investigations highlighted the relationship between PBIS implementation and reductions in disruptive behavior (Lewis et al., 1998; McCurdy et al., 2003; Tyre et al., 2011) and utilization of exclusionary discipline practices including office discipline referrals (Bradshaw et al., 2010), out-of-school suspensions (Bradshaw et al., 2010; Muscott et al., 2008), and out-of-school placements for students with significant behavioral needs (Freeman et al., 2006). Other work had supported the conclusion that high-fidelity PBIS implementation is associated with positive school climate and culture (Bradshaw et al., 2009), increased instructional time (Scott & Barrett, 2004), and academic improvements (Horner et al., 2009; Lassen et al., 2006; Luiselli et al., 2005; McIntosh et al., 2011; Muscott et al., 2008; Simonsen et al., 2012). While this evidence is certainly encouraging, such benefits may not be as pronounced for traditionally minoritized groups as they are for their White peers (McIntosh et al., 2018).

Hence, an important call within the field of PBIS is to discern the structures, policies, practices, and data to achieve equitable outcomes for all students.

Implementation Science

When planning for successful implementation of any program or initiative in a school, it is important to think of implementation as a process and not a singular event. This is true for MTSS for behavior and academics. Change does not happen immediately; rather, it occurs over time. Just as our understanding of how to implement MTSS has evolved over the years, so too has our understanding of implementation science for systems-level change.

Early work regarding implementation of MTSS for behavior (i.e., PBIS) identified three categorizations of implementation for a new school-wide initiative (Hume & McIntosh, 2013). Schools in the process of developing the infrastructure (e.g., policies, procedures, materials, training) to implement PBIS were categorized as *early adopters*. While many factors determine the duration of a school's status as an early adopter, typically such a designation lasts for about 1 year to 3 years. Once the initial excitement and energy for the initiative recedes and initial infrastructure building is completed, a school is designated as *low-sustaining*. This indicates that while the school has achieved initial implementation of the initiative, its longevity is precarious and requires continued commitment, in both human and financial capital, to sustain. Regrettably, it is during this phase that some schools abandon the initiative for any number of reasons including changes in leadership or prioritization, reduced funding, staff turnover, and burnout. Latham (1988) described these unfortunate scenarios as the 5-year life cycle of a typical school reform effort. However, if schools can sustain the initiative during the period of low-sustaining designation, when enthusiasm and energy wax and wane, they achieve what Hume and McIntosh (2013) categorize as *high-sustaining* implementation. Such a designation is marked by the initiative fully integrated into standard operating procedure. The initiative is no longer novel, unique, or innovative to staff; rather, the initiative is seamlessly integrated into daily practice.

Implementation science has evolved from this earlier work by acknowledging that there has to be an interest in learning about a new initiative prior to initial adoption. Consequently, contemporary implementation science identifies four discernable phases: Exploration, Installation, Initial Implementation, and Full Implementation (National Implementation Research Network, 2020). When school teams initiate the exploration phase, the overarching goals include assessing resources, needs, fit, and feasibility. During the exploration stage, it is important to engage stakeholders with diverse perspectives, including those not traditionally prioritized. Readiness for the initiative, program, or system is being developed and establishing communication processes and messages is essential. *The Hexagon: An Exploration Tool: Discussion and Analysis Guide* (Blasé et al., 2013) is an abundantly helpful resource to help schools evaluate potential programs or initiatives for adoption and determine fit and feasibility within their context (Runge et al., 2017). An essential outcome of the exploration phase is for the implementation team, representative of the school, to be formed and be ready to guide the work. Engaging members of the focus population and community partners when determining needs can help teams center equity from the start when programs and practices are considered for adoption.

A helpful resource from the National Implementation Research Network to guide schools through this process is the *Implementation Stages Planning Tool* (2020). It can be used at any stage of implementation to ensure that implementation efforts are matching the accurate stage of implementation for the practice or program. It includes the various activities and steps that should be taken during any stage of implementation to ensure essential infrastructure building, implementation, and sustainability practices are in place for the initiative.

Equity

When considering how to ensure equity through the implementation of MTSS or PBIS, a clear understanding of the contextual definition of equity must be established by the core team. This universal under-standing will be important to organize and coalesce around a shared vision and purpose.

According to The America's Promise Alliance, The Aspen Education and Society Program, and the Council of Chief State School Officers (2018), equity is defined as "every student has access to the educational resources and rigor they need at the right moment in their education across race, gender, ethnicity, language, disability, sexual orientation, family background and/or family income" (p. 5). This definition pro-vides a focus on the importance of access in the context of curriculum, technology, positive school climate, and physically safe learning envi-ronments. The "right moment" is indicative of the supports provided when student needs are demonstrated to create conditions for success and growth. A tiered system of supports is designed to establish and sustain a vehicle for equitable practices. Similar to MTSS, equity is not one-dimensional in scope. In education, equitable practices are inclu-sive of policy development, authentic family and community engage-ment, evaluation of data, culturally responsive and relevant academic practices, and disciplinary decisions that are supportive of inclusive learning environments. The intersection between PBIS and equity is a natural and necessary partnership to achieve many of the aforemen-tioned protective factors for student success.

Historical and Current Need for Equitable Disciplinary Practices

Inequitable application of exclusionary and punitive discipline policies has been well-documented in the United States since at least the 1970s (O'Connor et al., 2014). While several landmark pieces of legislation passed that showed promise of equitable educational opportunities for all students, there is still work to be done, especially in the area of disci-plinary practices. *Brown v. Board of Education* (1954) went to the Supreme Court, and the justices ruled unanimously that racial segregation of children in public schools was unconstitutional. This ruling helped set the precedent that "separate-but-equal" education and other services were inherently unequal. In 1975, Congress passed the Education for All

Handicapped Children Act (EAHCA; Public Law 94–142) requiring a free and appropriate public education for all students with disabilities. Prior to 1975, there were more than 4 million children and adolescents with disabilities who were denied access to an education. Revisions to EAHCA have occurred since the 1970s (Individuals with Disabilities Education Act [IDEA], 2004) with recent changes reflecting how the education of learners with disabilities can be made more effective via high-quality prevention and intervention offered through MTSS including "whole-school approaches, scientifically based early reading programs, positive behavioral interventions and supports, and early intervening services to reduce the need to label children as disabled in order to address the learning and behavioral needs of such children" (para. 9). In 2015, President Barack Obama signed into law the Every Student Succeeds Act (ESSA), the national education law dedicated to ensuring equal opportunity for all students, which includes references to MTSS five times.

Despite the efforts of legislation, serious issues continue to persist with the use of punitive and exclusionary disciplinary practices, especially for students with disabilities and students of color. To unpack the seriousness of this, it is important to understand why punitive and exclusionary discipline practices can be harmful. Student discipline issues are associated with numerous negative proximal and distal outcomes impacting students not only during their PreK–12 experience but also into adulthood. Short-term negative outcomes may include disruption to instructional time, decreased academic achievement, future disciplinary issues, and reduced graduation rates (e.g., Lee et al., 2011; McIntosh et al., 2006; Paine & Paine, 2002). Long-term negative outcomes can include involvement with law enforcement, incarceration, and unemployment/underemployment. McIntosh et al., (2006) conducted a longitudinal study, reviewing *Dynamic Indicators of Basic Early Literacy Skills* and office discipline referral (ODR) data for a cohort of students from their kindergarten through fifth grade years. An interaction between reading skills and problem behavior was indicated with both reading skill level and ODRs in earlier grades significantly predicting ODRs in fifth grade. Lee et al., (2011) examined data from 289 high schools in Virginia and found schools with high suspension rates (i.e., 22% of students received suspension over a school year) had a 56% greater dropout rate than schools with low suspension rates (i.e., 9% or less of students received suspension during a school year).

Discipline issues in school are also associated with long-term negative outcomes for students including increased likelihood for involvement with law enforcement, incarceration, poor employment outcomes, and adverse economic impacts (e.g., Bullis & Yovanoff, 2006; Zigmond, 2006). In their study, Bullis and Yovanoff (2006) followed 531 juveniles, who were incarcerated, after they transitioned from a facility to the community. Nearly 58% of the sample had been identified with an educational disability, with the majority of those being an emotional disturbance (29.9%), an educational disability that, by definition, may include inappropriate types of behaviors. Significantly lower employment rates were indicated for the individuals with emotional disturbance and other educational disabilities than for the individuals without educational disabilities. Zigmond (2006) evaluated employment outcomes 24 months after graduation from high school for students who had demonstrated social, emotional, and behavioral problems in school and had been labeled as having an educational disability of emotional disturbance. Only 60% of those students were employed 24 months after graduation. The majority of these individuals had inconsistency in their employment, drifting in and out of jobs. Additionally, students who attended post-secondary training also drifted in and out of training programs, and for those who completed such a program, significant increases in income were not realized.

It is important for school teams to understand disproportionate practices in discipline have been documented in the literature for many years, and it is possible their school may be engaging in disproportionate disciplinary practices. School disciplinary policies and procedures, including how problem behaviors are defined as well as the types of consequences administered for inappropriate behavior, can vary greatly across schools and districts. School teams installing, implementing, and sustaining PBIS must be aware of disproportionate patterns of discipline so they can work to disrupt those practices and prevent them from occurring.

Disproportionate disciplinary practices have been indicated across gender, socioeconomic status, race, ability status, and sexual orientation. Disproportionality has also been identified in other demographic characteristics which may include special education placement or gifted placement. Contextually, disproportionality may occur related to access, whether that is through less funding, less advanced placement course options, or less extracurricular activities. An evaluation of longitudinal suspension data for the state of Maryland indicated disproportionality in suspensions with minority students and students with disabilities being suspended at disproportionately higher rates. Specific intersectionality was noted for Black students with emotional and behavioral disabilities placing them at the highest risk for suspension (Krezmien et al., 2006). Skiba and colleagues (2002) evaluated gender, race, and socioeconomic status in disciplinary practices, finding that Black students were significantly more likely to be disciplined for behaviors that were more subjective in nature (e.g., disrespect, noise) whereas White students were disciplined for more objective and observable behaviors such as smoking and leaving without permission. When considering intersectionality of race, gender, and disability status, Black males with disabilities are at highest risk with approximately one-third being suspended at least one time per academic year (United States Department of Education, Office for Civil Rights, 2014).

Despite the abundance of historical and current research on the adverse outcomes associated with punitive and exclusionary discipline practices, these practices are still widespread across the country and often at disproportionate rates for different groups of students. Data practices can help schools identify any groups of students at-risk of being impacted by punitive and exclusionary disciplinary practices at disproportionate rates. These practices are also critical to detecting other inequities that extend beyond discipline. Once data have been identified, collected, and analyzed, then practices, policies, and processes can be modified to address the inequities while data are monitored to determine if those modifications facilitated more equitable opportunities, access and outcomes.

The purpose of this resource is to help school teams address these issues through the establishment and implementation of an equitable and effective PBIS framework to serve all students through an equity mindset. Data and practices should be at the forefront of development and implementation to ensure equitable outcomes for every student. This is particularly relevant given the ever-increasing diversity of U.S. schools and growing evidence of disproportionate outcomes for marginalized and minoritized groups.

As you navigate the remaining chapters of our book, we encourage you to review the "seeds for growth" as key takeaways, as well as the vignettes/scenarios from fictional schools at the end of each chapter. These have been included as a way to humanize this important work and to validate any roadblocks you and your team may experience in the implementation journey. Additionally, each chapter offers reproducible templates/samples to support your team's ongoing efforts and to reduce the need to *start from scratch*. While these examples and templates speak to our experiences with schools, we understand the need for you to contextualize the information we offer to your respective settings. The work of EIB is highly based on the makeup of your system and the individuals who comprise it. Our goal for you and your team as you engage in this text is to establish shared learning, understand the importance of honoring a process and not a destination, and center those who have been most impacted by disproportionate outcomes. The next chapter takes you to the first step of equitable implementation of PBIS by *beginning the journey*. We hope you enjoy your next stop.

Chapter 1: Seeds for Growth

- ◆ PBIS is not a curriculum, but a **multi-tiered framework** for organizing assessments, resources, interventions, and supports for all students in an **efficient** and **effective** manner.
- ◆ The comprehensive, three-tiered PBIS model provides the organizational framework, including assessment, data collection and analysis, and resource deployment structures, to then embed **culturally relevant, evidence-based interventions** that meet the needs of students in the school.

- A tiered system of support is designed to establish and sustain a vehicle for equitable practices. Similar to multi-tiered systems of support, **equity** is not one-dimensional in scope.
- It is important for school teams to understand **disproportionate practices** in access, opportunities and outcomes discipline have been documented in the literature for many years, and it is possible their school **may be** engaging in disproportionate disciplinary practices.
- **Data** and **practices** should be at the forefront of development and implementation to ensure equitable outcomes for all students.

Vignette/Example

The Graystone Mountain School District is known across the state as a high-performing suburban school district with an enrollment of approximately 7,000 students. The district offers many extracurricular opportunities to meet a wide variety of student interests. Faculty and staff retention rates are very high. Many individuals who begin their careers in education at Graystone Mountain School District remain for the duration of their career and retire from the district. The district has an active parent teacher organization as well as strong connections with the community. Many families want to live within the geographic boundaries of the Graystone Mountain School District because of the strong education system and abundant opportunities for students that exist within the district.

On a recent state department of education mandated compliance monitoring audit of special education practices, Graystone Mountain School District received several citations for which corrective action steps were assigned. First, the district special education identification rates reflected significant disproportionality for students of color, particularly Hispanic/Latino/a/x and Black/African American students. The district's student racial and ethnic population was comprised of the following percentages: Asian: 2%, Black/African American: 5%, Hispanic/Latino/a/x: 6%, White: 82%, Multi-Racial: 5%.

With regard to special education services district-wide, 15% of all students were identified with a disability for which they had an Individualized Education Program (IEP). Further analysis of special education eligibility data found that across all special education categories defined by the IDEA (2004), 40% of all students with disabilities were from minoritized demographic groups. When reviewing data from each of the IDEA eligibility categories, additional disproportionate representation was indicated. Hispanic/Latino/a/x students comprised 22% of all students identified with a specific learning disability, despite only being 6% of the student population. Likewise, when the eligibility category of emotional disturbance was analyzed for potential disproportionality, data reflected Black/African American students represented 31% of students identified with emotional disturbance, despite being only 5% of the student population in the district.

The results of the state department of education special education audit served as a catalyst for the Graystone Mountain School District's administrative team to first begin reflecting upon the systems in place that were potentially contributing to a higher risk of adverse outcomes for students of color, particularly Hispanic/Latino/a/x and Black/African American students. While the administrative team members initially believed the district provided equitable opportunities for every student, the data offered another perspective. This was the starting point for the Graystone Mountain School District's journey. The administrative team determined they needed to engage in self and systems reflection, then explore evidence-based frameworks and action steps to improve outcomes for every student.

Reference List

America's Promise Alliance, A. E. a. S. P., and the Council of Chief State School Officers. (2018). *States leading for equity*. Author.

Blasé, K., Kiser, L., & Van Dyke, M. (2013). *The hexagon tool: Exploring context*. National Implementation Research Network, FPG Child Development Institute, University of North Carolina at Chapel Hill.

Bradshaw, C. P., Koth, C. W., Thornton, L. A., & Leaf, P. J. (2009). Altering school climate through school-wide positive behavioral interventions and supports: Findings from a group-randomized effectiveness trial. *Prevention Science, 10*(2), 100–115. doi:10.1007/s11121-008-0114-9

Bradshaw, C. P., Mitchell, M. M., & Leaf, P. J. (2010). Examining the effects of schoolwide positive behavioral interventions and supports on student outcomes: Results from a randomized controlled effectiveness trial in elementary schools. *Journal of Positive Behavior Interventions, 12*(3), 133–149. doi:10.1177/1098300709334798

Brown v. Board of Education, 347 U.S. 483. (1954).

Bullis, M., & Yovanoff, P. (2006). Idle hands: Community employment experiences of formerly incarcerated youth. *Journal of Emotional and Behavioral Disorders, 14*, 71–85.

Eber, L., Hyde, K., & Suter, J. C. (2011). Integrating wraparound into a schoolwide system of positive behavior supports. *Journal of Child and Family Studies, 20*, 782–790.

Essential Components of MTSS. (n.d.) *Center on multi-tiered systems of support at the American institutes of research.* https://mtss4success.org/essential-components

Freeman, R., Eber, L., Anderson, C., Irvin, L., Horner, R., Bounds, M., & Dunlap, G. (2006). Building inclusive school cultures using school-wide pbs: Designing effective individual support systems for students with significant disabilities. *Research & Practice for Persons with Severe Disabilities, 31*(1), 4–17.

Gottfredson, G. D., & Gottfredson, D. C. (1996). *A national study of delinquency prevention in schools: Rationale for a study to describe the extensiveness and implementation of programs to prevent adolescent problem behavior in schools.* Gottfredson Associates.

Heidelberg, K., Rutherford, L., & Parks, T. W. (2022). A preliminary analysis assessing SWPBIS implementation fidelity in relation to disciplinary outcomes of black students in urban schools. *The Urban Review, 54*(3), 138–154. https://doi.org/10.1007/s11256-021-00609

Horner, R., Sugai, G., Smolkowski, K., Eber, L., Nakasato, J., Todd, A., & Esperanza, J. (2009). A randomized, wait-list controlled effectiveness trial assessing school-wide positive behavior support in elementary schools. *Journal of Positive Behavior Interventions, 11*(3), 133–145.

Hume, A., & McIntosh, K. (2013). Construct validation of a measure to assess sustainability of school-wide behavior interventions. *Psychology in the Schools, 50,* 1003–1014. doi:10.1002/pits.21722.

Individuals with Disabilities Education Act, 20 U.S.C. § 602. (2004).

Kincaid, D., Dunlap, G., Kern, L., Lane, K. L., Bambara, L. M., Brown, F., Fox, L., Knoster, T. P. (2016, April). Positive behavior support: A proposal for updating and refining the definition. *Journal of Positive Behavior Interventions, 18*(2), 69–73.

Krezmien, M. P., Leone, M. P., & Achilles, G. M. (2006). Suspension, race and disability: Analysis of statewide practices and reporting. *Journal of Emotional and Behavioral Disorders, 14*(4), 217–226.

Lassen, S. R., Steele, M. M., & Sailor, W. (2006). The relationship of school-wide positive behavior support to academic achievement in an urban middle school. *Psychology in the Schools, 43*(6), 701–712. doi:10.1002/pits.20177

Latham, G. (1988). The birth and death cycles of educational innovations. *Principal, 68*(1), 41–43.

Lee, T., Cornell, D., Gregory, A., & Xitao, F. (2011). High suspension schools and dropout rates for black and white students. In *Education & treatment of children* (pp. 167–192). West Virginia University Press. doi:10.1353/etc.2011.0014

Lewis, T. J., Sugai, G., & Colvin, G. (1998). Reducing problem behavior through a school-wide system of effective behavioral support: Investigation of a school-wide social skills training program and contextual intervention. *School Psychology Review, 27*(3), 446–459.

Luiselli, J. K., Putnam, R. F., Handler, M. W., & Feinberg, A. B. (2005). Whole-school positive behaviour support: Effects on student discipline problems and academic performance. *Educational Psychology, 25*(2), 183–198. doi:10.1080/0144341042000301265

McCurdy, B. L., Mannella, M. C., & Eldridge, N. (2003). Positive behavior support in urban schools: Can we prevent the escalation of antisocial behavior? *Journal of Positive Behavior Interventions, 5*(3), 158–170. doi:10.1177/10983007030050030501

McIntosh, K., Bennett, J. L., & Price, K. (2011). Evaluation of social and academic effects of school-wide positive behavior support in a Canadian school district. *Exceptionality Education International, 21*(1), 46–60. doi:10.5206/eei.v21i1.7669

McIntosh, K., Gion, C., & Bastable, E. (2018). *Do schools implementing SWPBIS have decreased racial and ethnic disproportionality in school discipline?* Office of Special Education Programs, National Technical Assistance Center on Positive Behavior Support. pbis.org.

McIntosh, K., Horner, R. H., Chard, D. J., Boland, B., & Good, R. H. (2006). The use of reading and behavior screening measures to predict non-response to school wide positive behavior support: A longitudinal analysis. *School Psychology Review, 35*, 275–291.

Muscott, H. S., Mann, E. L., & LeBrun, M. R. (2008). Positive behavioral interventions and support in new hampshire: Effects of large-scale implementation of schoolwide positive behavior support on student discipline and academic achievement. *Journal of Positive Behavior Interventions, 10*(3), 190–205. doi:10.1177/1098300708316258

National Implementation Research Network. (2020). *Implementation stages planning tool.* National Implementation Research Network, FPG Child Development Institute, University of North Carolina at Chapel Hill.

O'Conner, R., Porowski, A., & Passa, A. (2014). *Disproportionality in school discipline: An assessment of trends in Maryland, 2009–12 (REL 2013–033).* U.S. Department of Education, Institute of Education Sciences, National Center for Education Evaluation and Regional Assistance, Regional Educational Laboratory Mid-Atlantic. http://ies.ed.gov/ncee/edlabs.

Paine, S., & Paine, C. K. (2002). Promoting safety and success in school by developing students' strengths. In M. R. Shinn, G. Stoner, & H. M. Walker (Eds.), *Interventions for academic and behavior problems: Preventive and remedial approaches* (pp. 89–108). National Association of School Psychologists.

Pennsylvania Training and Technical Assistance Network. (2018). *Response to intervention.* https://www.pattan.net/Multi-Tiered-System-of-Support/Response-to-Intervention-RTI

Runge, T. J., Knoster, T. P., Moerer, D., Breinich, T., & Palmiero, J. (2017). A practical protocol for situating mental health evidence-based and promising programs and practices within the positive behavioral interventions and supports. *Advances in School Mental Health Promotion, 10*(2), 1–12. doi:10.1080/1754730X.2017.1285708

Runge, T. J., Staszkiewicz, M. J., Bardo, A. E., Myers, T., Breon, S., & Kozel, M. (2021). *12th annual executive summary of the Pennsylvania positive behavior support network's implementation of school-wide positive behavioral interventions and supports.* Indiana University of Pennsylvania.

Scott, T. M., & Barrett, S. B. (2004). Using staff and student time engaged in disciplinary procedures to evaluate the impact of school-wide pbs. *Journal of Positive Behavior Interventions, 6*(1), 21–27. doi:10.1177/10983007040060010401

Simonsen, B., Eber, L., Black, A. C., Sugai, G., Lewandowski, H., Sims, B., & Myers, D. (2012). Illinois statewide positive behavioral interventions and supports: Evolution and impact on student outcomes across years. *Journal of Positive Behavior Interventions, 14*(1), 5–16. doi:10.1177/1098300711412601

Skiba, R. J., Michael, R. S., Nardo, A. C., & Peterson, R. L. (2002). The color of discipline: Sources of racial and gender disproportionality in school punishment. *The Urban Review, 34*(4), 317–342.

Sugai, G., & Horner, R. H. (2009). Schoolwide positive behavior support. In W. Sailor, G. Sugai, G. Dunlap, & R. H. Horner (Eds.), *Handbook of positive behavior support* (pp. 307–326). Springer Science + Media.

Sugai, G., & Horner, R. H. (2014). Positive behavior support, school-wide. In C. R. Reynolds, K. J. Vannest, & E. Fletcher-Janzen (Eds.), *Encyclopedia of special education: A reference for the education of children, adolescents, and adults with disabilities and other exceptionalities.* John Wiley & Sons. https://doi.org/10.1002/9781118660584.ese1902

Tyre, A., Feuerborn, L., & Pierce, J. (2011). Schoolwide intervention to reduce chronic tardiness at the middle and high school levels. *Preventing School Failure, 55*(3), 132–139. doi:10.1080/10459880903472918

U.S. Department of Education, Office of Civil Rights. (2014). *Civil rights data collection (CRDC), 2009 to 2010 [Data set].* http://ocrdata.ed.gov/

Walker, H. M., Ramsey, E., & Gresham, F. M. (2005). *Antisocial behavior in schools: Evidence- based practices* (2nd ed.). Wadsworth/Thomson Learning.

Zigmond, N. (2006). Twenty-four months after high school: Paths taken by youth diagnosed with severe emotional and behavioral disorders. *Journal of Emotional and Behavioral Disorders, 14*, 99–107.

Readiness Quick-Check

As you take the next steps of creating equitable PBIS systems, please consider your current status with regard to discipline and school climate. The following quick-check can support you as you consider the need for a comprehensive framework that supports every learner. Perhaps your team is already implementing PBIS with fidelity and some of these items may not apply. However, there may be items here that suggest your infrastructure may benefit from enhancements.

- ◆ Do you have a challenge in your school/district related to school climate or discipline?
    - – Inappropriate behaviors
    - – Low staff morale
    - – State regulated corrective action regarding disproportionality
    - – Student arrests
    - – Alternative education placement increases
    - – Special education identification increases for emotional/behavioral disorders
- ◆ How have you addressed these challenges?
    - – Purchased behavior programs
    - – Created a space in the building for students with behavior concerns to *cool down*
    - – Removed points or activities based on student behavior
    - – Sent students home when behaviors escalate
    - – Partnered with community organizations/after-school programs to support the school's efforts, but not consistently

- Connected with mental health providers as additional supports between school and community, but not consistently
◆ What would you need to make your system a space of belonging for every learner?
  - Authentic partnerships with families and community organizations
  - Dedicated professional learning for staff
  - Student advisory groups
  - Indicators of success—data to tell us if we are on the right track
  - Shared ownership of students with intensive academic, behavioral, or emotional challenges
  - A school community willing to create and sustain positive change

If you are finding that most of the items listed in the Readiness Quick-Check match your current experience, then this text will be a valuable resource to your journey of creating conditions of an equitable PBIS system. PBIS is not a program but rather a comprehensive and sustainable framework driven by data, systems, practices, and outcomes and is centered in equity. With equity at the core, inclusion and belonging are natural next steps and have the potential to improve the educational experiences of students and staff, while also positively impacting communities.

2

Beginning the Journey

The Journey Begins With a Team

Where does the journey to equitable and effective implementation of positive behavioral interventions and supports (PBIS) begin? The journey begins with a team to plan for installation, initial implementation, full implementation, and sustainability of PBIS. A number of different teams already exist within school structures including district-level, school-level, grade-level, and department-level teams and even student teams, each with their own focus and set of responsibilities. Throughout the teaming structures, cross-team representation should exist in some capacity for consistency and efficiency of implementation district wide. The integration of effective academic and PBIS practices is essential as teams look at data, systems, and practices to meet the needs of every student (McIntosh & Goodman, 2016). What teaming structures are needed for equitable and effective PBIS? How might existing teams be leveraged and transformed to support PBIS?

Having a consistent vision and necessary support for PBIS is essential at the highest level of the school organization. Membership on a district-level team might include district- and school-level administrators, community representatives, family representatives, coordinators or coaches of multi-tiered system of supports (MTSS) from each school

DOI: 10.4324/9781003294351-2

building, and student representation. The primary functions of this team can include tasks to build and sustain district-wide support and infrastructure for an integrated MTSS, evaluate district efforts and outcomes, measure fidelity of implementation, and develop district action plans for continuous improvement and sustainability. The emphasis is on building and sustaining systems capacity.

A school-level tier 1 PBIS leadership team is critical for effective implementation. It is important to consider the core competencies needed for an effective team and individuals who possess those skills when determining membership. Administrative authority to ensure actions can be implemented, behavioral expertise, instructional expertise, and family, student, and community voice are all essential to inform PBIS implementation. An administrator who is able to support and ensure resources, policies, and practices are allocated to implement and sustain PBIS is required. Administrative support is an essential factor in the establishment and initial implementation of PBIS (McIntosh et al., 2013; Pinkelman et al., 2018). An individual with training and expertise in effective behavioral practices such as a school psychologist, school counselor, school social worker, behavioral specialist, or board certified behavior analyst (BCBA) is another essential member of the team to help guide problem-solving and ensure action steps are aligned to evidence-based positive behavioral support practices. Grade and department-level representation is essential to bring perspective regarding classroom practices. Other educational professionals, community members, and family representatives also bring valuable insight to the school PBIS leadership team. A speech and language pathologist trained in assessment and supporting student communication skills can contribute to the problem-solving process, while a paraeducator may bring firsthand experience with supporting students with complex disabilities in the classroom. A community representative from a local mental health provider would contribute additional expertise on mental health and available community resources. Faith-based leaders have knowledge of belief systems and local culture; they often provide a valued source of support for many families and children. Local business representatives can contribute to PBIS efforts, perhaps by donating services or products or even by displaying PBIS expectations in their local business where students and families visit. Partnership with civic organizations can help strengthen connections between the school and community. Support provided by community members can be integrated within the PBIS framework. For example, perhaps each month a different community organization sponsors a PBIS activity for the students and staff. Finally, family representation on the core PBIS leadership team is critical. Family representatives can contribute by sharing their perspectives to inform contextual fit with family and community values in PBIS implementation, as well as mobilizing parent groups to assist and partner in PBIS.

The school-level tier 1 team serves several important purposes. A school-level tier 1 team oversees the implementation at the school building, including reviewing data, at minimum, monthly to drive decision making. Additional functions of the school-level team include developing necessary building infrastructure to support PBIS at the school level, establishment and implementation of systems-level practices, communication with all staff, and providing professional development and support around PBIS implementation. Additionally, monitoring fidelity and analyzing behavioral and academic data are essential roles of the PBIS school-level team to sustain PBIS implementation.

Grade-level and department-level teams are an essential extension of the building-level tier 1 team. At an elementary school it may be more common to see grade-level teams, while at the middle and high school levels it may be more common to see department-level teams. Membership includes all teachers for a particular grade level (e.g., second grade) or for a specific department (e.g., math department). These team members are closest to classroom practices and provide insight and expertise on PBIS applied at the classroom level. While there is grade-level and department-level representation on the tier 1 PBIS leadership team, those representatives serve as a liaison to their respective grade-level or department-level colleagues to communicate information from the tier 1 PBIS leadership team and to solicit feedback and input to share in return. It may also be helpful to have administrative support at grade-level teams to aid in decisions requiring administrative authority.

Student representation, especially for middle and high school aged students, is essential in informing practices and policies. There are multiple ways to facilitate meaningful and authentic student involvement. First, including student representatives on district-level and school-level teams is a way to incorporate authentic student voice and perspective in policies and practices. Second, schools should consider establishing student school-level PBIS leadership teams that work in tandem with the adult school-level PBIS teams. The student PBIS team, representative of the student body, can provide valuable input into policies and practices. It is important to include representation from all student demographic and social groups represented in the school's population on the student PBIS team. Representation matters; if the student PBIS team is homogenous in its membership (i.e., similar demographically, similar social group), other groups of students may not see PBIS as something for them because they have no representation on the team. For young students, there are meaningful ways to include their voices in PBIS. Student teams could be considered, depending upon student age. Young students could be asked to vote on choices for components of PBIS, such as a choice of incentives, with the data from their voting displayed and their preferences implemented. Students might be given their own tickets so they might acknowledge other students or adults to positively reinforce individuals displaying PBIS expected behaviors. Students of any age might provide input on expectations for positive behavior in student-friendly language or even be involved in the development of videos and lessons modeling expected behaviors. Student teams will need some training, guidance, and an avenue to have their voice not only be heard but also to have their ideas implemented. Student voice complements SWPBIS and is essential for improving the social climate of the school (O'Malley et al., 2014).

Students in middle and high schools can provide firsthand perspective on aggregate data sources they review, such as answering potential "why" questions. For example, when reviewing attendance and tardy data, adults may hypothesize that increases in morning tardies for 11th and 12th grade students may be due to students being tired from staying up late and choosing to sleep later in the morning. Students, however, know there is a café 15 minutes away and that juniors and seniors are going to the café before school to eat delicious breakfasts. Students know this is becoming an increasingly popular thing for juniors and seniors to do before school. As a result of student input, solution actions for identified problems may then be better targeted to address the root cause (e.g., work out an agreement with the café to provide selected items at the high school for breakfast 2 days a week) than the adults' solutions for the identified problem (e.g., educational videos on getting a good night's sleep and reinforcing on-time arrivals). By positioning students in a leadership role in PBIS, students can help lead the way to creating safe, supportive, consistent, positive, and equitable school environments for everyone.

How do teams organize supports for students who have needs that tier 1 does not fully address? Planning for the delivery of strategic and intensive supports by an advanced tiers team involves a different type of team structure, membership, and focus. Advanced tiers teams meet more frequently (e.g., 2x a month) than the tier 1 team. Membership includes individuals with behavioral expertise (e.g., school psychologist, school counselor, school social worker, behavioral specialist), an administrator, special education teachers, support personnel, content specialists, and district personnel (as needed). These teams tend to be smaller in membership (e.g., 6–8 members) because they are problem-solving around small groups of students with a similar type of need or individual students. Advanced tiers teams (or problem-solving teams) serve functions including establishing of infrastructure to support students in need of strategic or intensive (i.e., tier 2 or tier 3) intervention and coordination and management of advanced tiers interventions. This team designs, monitors, and evaluates fidelity and communicates effectiveness of interventions at advanced tiers. Just as it is important for tier 1 support to meet the needs of a large percentage of students (i.e., 80%–85%), tier 2 and 3 supports should be effective for 80% or more of students enrolled in those supports.

When the problem-solving focuses efforts to support an individual student, involvement of family members and caregivers is an essential part of the problem-solving process. The individual student problem-solving team members may include the administrator; student; family members/caregivers; student's classroom teacher(s); content specialists (e.g., reading specialist); related service providers as appropriate (e.g., speech and language pathologist); other problem-solving team members specializing in social, emotional, and behavioral supports (e.g., school psychologist, behavior specialist, community mental health partner); English as a second language (ESL) or teachers of English learners; and others as needed. This team meets at minimum yearly or more frequently, as needed. The purpose of this team is to collect and analyze student-level data, develop individualized interventions and supports matched to need, and review student progress toward goals.

Scenario

The ABCD School District, a suburban district with an enrollment of approximately 4,500 students, received a large grant to improve school safety. Stakeholders involved in writing the grant placed an emphasis on improving preventative approaches for the use of their funds and scope of the work. They explored potential systems-level approaches and decided that installation of PBIS district-wide would provide a comprehensive framework and could be contextualized to meet the needs of the school district community. Included in the grant proposal was a job description and a plan to hire a school psychologist to serve in an innovative systems-level role as District Coordinator of PBIS. An essential role of the District Coordinator of PBIS was to provide systems and content coaching to improve the coordinated capacity of teams of educators to implement and sustain PBIS with fidelity.

The first task of the District Coordinator of PBIS was to facilitate the establishment of implementation teams at the district and school levels to drive the implementation process. The process started by auditing existing district-level and school-level teams: determining the purpose of the team, membership, meeting frequency, decisions made by the team, meeting protocol, alignment to the district's mission and goals, and outcomes of the teaming process. By auditing existing school teams, this made it possible to determine if any existing teams could be repurposed or its focus adjusted to support PBIS. Additionally, this provided an opportunity to see if any team's purposes overlapped or their efforts were duplicated in some manner. This was a necessary step before forming more teams, adding more meetings, and creating potential duplicity to educators' already full workloads. The District Coordinator of PBIS used the *Working Smarter Matrix: Committee and Group Self-Assessment* (Sugai, 2010) as a resource to support this process.

After review of the audit, the District Coordinator of PBIS worked at the district and school level to repurpose and help several existing teams adjust their focus, as well as establish the new teams needed for PBIS implementation. (The *Checklist for Considerations for PBIS Team Membership* can assist with this process.) For example, when auditing existing teams, it was determined that a team already existed at each of the buildings to problem-solve about students whom teachers or parents had concerns. These existing teams already included necessary membership for advanced tiers teams. Including behavioral data from core PBIS and advanced tiers interventions and supports integrated in the PBIS framework enhanced the existing process.

After ensuring all necessary teams were established or existing teams were able to adjust their focus to include supporting PBIS installation and implementation, the District Coordinator of PBIS recognized that every team had different ways of facilitating meetings and looking at data (if data were reviewed at all). This can be problematic for effective implementation. When meetings lack effective practices, effective decisions are less likely to be made and valuable resources (e.g., staff time) are wasted. The next step on the ABCD School District's journey was to investigate and install an effective meeting process to support data-based decision making.

Team-Initiated Problem-Solving Process

How might these various teams most effectively and efficiently spend their meeting time with a focus on data-based decision-making and problem solving? Team-Initiated Problem Solving (TIPS) is a research-validated framework to support effective and efficient data-based team decision-making applicable to a variety of data sources (e.g., ODR data; attendance data; academic data such as Acadience, DIBELS, AIMSWeb, SpringMath, etc.; Horner et al., 2015). The TIPS process includes meeting foundations to ensure teams have essential components in place, such as meeting schedules, required attendance, agendas, and assigned roles for team members. The defined team roles include facilitator, note taker, data analyst, and team member, with each role having specific responsibilities to ensure meetings are effective and lead to actionable items for implementation. The TIPS process includes structured meeting minutes to organize team meetings and facilitate effective problem-solving based upon data. Finally, TIPS includes a problem-solving process to help teams identify a problem with precision, based upon data, identify a goal for change, identify solutions to address the identified problem, implement and monitor the efficacy and fidelity of the solution, and make summative evaluative decisions (Horner et al., 2015).

Self and System Awareness

It is essential that team members start their journey together with an audit of self-awareness. Self-awareness can be described as a reflective consciousness of how we understand the impact of our implicit thoughts, feelings, and behaviors. Identity is a concept that often influences how we interpret or relate to others. Social identities are those pieces of ourselves which impact how we view others, who and what we value, where we find commonality and understanding, and who we see as different. Those who are seen as different may also be viewed with a deficit-mindset dependent upon our preconceived views of their backgrounds or media-driven stereotypes (Payno-Simmons, 2021). Team members need to develop an understanding of not only their own individual identities but also be able to reflect upon systems and determine the values of the system. For example, does the system have low expectations for particular groups of students but high expectations for other groups of students? These concepts of self and system awareness will be addressed in further depth with helpful tips and resources for facilitation in Chapter 4. While self and system awareness are paramount to ensuring equitable approaches are viable, this process may initially start with data practices.

Data Practices

Data, systems, and practices are implemented and reviewed regularly by PBIS leadership teams to ensure desired and equitable outcomes. Evaluating a variety of available data sources can help teams shape systems and practices to improve outcomes for every student. There are many sources of data already available in schools that teams can leverage to guide their efforts. Here common data sources leadership teams can access to guide systems and practices to enhance outcomes are highlighted.

Discipline Data

One of the most common sources of data collected by schools is Office Discipline Referral (ODR) data. An ODR is a systematic documentation of a student behavior problem (Sugai et al., 2000). An ODR provides information about the incident such as location, time of day, description of problem behavior/incident, individuals involved, and perceived motivation (e.g., to gain or avoid attention, tangibles, activities). Consequences for student misbehavior or misconduct such as disciplinary action including detention, out-of-school or in-school suspension, or expulsion may often be the results of ODRs. Teachers often generate ODRs; school administrators typically are the individuals responsible for assigning follow-up actions associated with the ODR documentation. Gaining in popularity with school districts as measures of problem behavior, ODRs are accessible and useful in making decisions at the school and individual level (McIntosh et al., 2009).

As highlighted earlier in Chapter 1, there are a host of negative outcomes associated with ODRs (e.g., Bullis & Yovanoff, 2006; Lee et al., 2011; McIntosh et al., 2006; Paine & Paine, 2002). Discipline issues in school are also associated with long-term negative outcomes for students. These can include increased likelihood for involvement with law enforcement, incarceration, and poor employment outcomes (e.g., Bullis & Yovanoff, 2006). The stakes are higher when exclusion from school (e.g., suspension) is an administrative action taken as a result of an ODR. Even a single suspension in 9th grade decreases the likelihood a student will graduate high school or attend college (Balfanz et al.,

2014). As mentioned in Chapter 1, disproportionality in disciplinary actions resulting from ODRs has been noted. Black students and Latinx students were found to be more likely than their White peers to receive expulsion or out-of-school suspension as consequences for the same or similar problem behaviors (Skiba et al., 2011). While one of the outcomes associated with fidelity PBIS has been a reduction in ODRs, that is not the case for all student groups. Heidelberg et al., (2022) found no relationship between fidelity implementation and total ODRs for Black students in urban elementary and middle schools. It is imperative that PBIS leadership teams are skilled in disaggregation of data for marginalized and minoritized groups to determine whether and where problems rest, how to potentially intervene on those problems, how to establish ambitious goals, and how to evaluate the extent to which established goals for improvement have been met.

Ensuring PBIS is working for most students is a necessary starting point. An indication of healthy tier 1 instruction and support occurs when approximately 80% to 90% of students receive no or one ODR in an academic year, in secondary and elementary schools, respectively (SWIS, 2019). Of students who have 0–1 ODR, with such proportions being larger at the elementary grades, it can be assumed their needs are being met through tier 1 instruction and support. Students who receive two or more ODRs are those who need advanced tiers of support to be successful. Students who receive two ODRs by October have a high likelihood to accumulate six or more ODRs by the end of the school year (McIntosh et al., 2010) if additional supports are not provided.

After evaluating the efficacy of tier 1 instruction and support, teams must be able to look more closely at data for students whose needs are not met by tier 1. Teams need to know if tier 1 supports meet the needs of most students in the school. In addition, teams need to know if tier 1 meets the needs of most students in every subgroup in the school's population. For example, if tier 1 meets the needs of 85% of the entire student population but only meets the needs of 10% of the subgroup of English learners included in the student population, tier 1 is not effective for the school's subgroup of English learners. It is essential that teams know how to disaggregate data and evaluate for disproportionate outcomes across all marginalized and minoritized student groups, given adverse outcomes associated with ODRs. Additionally, teams will want to disaggregate data and evaluate for disproportionate outcomes for groups of students receiving 2–5 ODRs and six or more ODRs, as these cut points signify need for targeted and intensive intervention, respectively (McIntosh et al., 2009). Detailed information on how to disaggregate data and calculate risk indices and risk ratios to facilitate equitable decision-making is reviewed in Chapter 3.

Academic Data

There are many sources of academic data that can, and should, be reviewed in tandem with ODRs and other behavioral data sources. Teams should start with data to which they already have access given schools have various extant data collected for other decision-making purposes. For example, teams should have access to summative, accountability data (e.g., year-end state testing results) and can generate reports of percentages of students reaching proficiency on key academic skills. Triannual academic screening data, with assessments having adequate psychometric properties to accurately identify risk and measure growth over time (e.g., Acadience, Aimsweb Plus, Spring-Math, STAR, and others) can provide valuable insight with regard to percentages of students meeting benchmarks on the path to proficiency in literacy and/or mathematics. Teams can learn more about purposes, features, and technical adequacy of universal screeners for academics at www.rtinetwork.org/learn/research/universal-screening-within-a-rti-model from the RTI Action Network from the National Center on Learning Disabilities (Hughes & Dexter, 2022). The National Center on Intensive Intervention provides an open-access online site teams can explore to compare various academic screening tools that have been independently reviewed (2021). Information is provided on features such as classification accuracy, technical standards, and usability via the Academic Screening Tools Chart comparison found at https://charts.intensiveintervention.org/ascreening.

Academic data are intricately intertwined with ODR data. For example, when ODR data are analyzed and found to be occurring at heightened level during academic subjects (e.g., reading/language arts, mathematics) teams must ask more questions to generate a precision statement to accurately get to the root cause. The root cause may not be purely "behavioral" in nature; rather, teams must ask if students are being provided with evidence-based, standards-aligned core instruction matched to their instructional level, including high levels of student engagement. For example, if an elementary school implements whole language or balanced literacy approaches for reading, the PBIS leadership team may notice reading screening data that reflect large percentages of students not on track for meeting basic early literacy skills. As a result, teachers may observe students engaging in off-task, mildly disruptive behaviors during reading instruction because of the instructional mismatch resulting in student frustration given the absence of explicit, systematic instruction in basic reading skills. In this instance, reteaching students behavioral expectations and providing them with reinforcement would be insufficient at addressing issues with academic instruction. Instead, the installation of scientifically based curricula and evidence-based instructional practices would likely ameliorate many of the perceived misbehaviors of students in those classrooms.

Scenario

The school-level tier 1 team at North Side Elementary School meets monthly to review building-level data. The team recognized that in November a high number of ODRs were occurring (i.e., a rate of 12 ODRs per day); disruptive behaviors were most common in classrooms were where most ODRs were used, and ODRs occurred across all grade levels and throughout the day. The team's first precision statement for problem-solving using the data was as follows: "Students in kindergarten, 1st grade, 2nd grade, and 3rd grade are engaging in disruptive behaviors (talking out, out of seat) in the classroom during whole group and independent practice activities at a rate of 12 ODRs per day in order to gain adult attention." As a result, the school-level tier 1 team generated a solution action to increase positive adult attention when students were engaged by providing a minimum of one PBIS ticket per student per class period when that student was engaged in the assigned task. Teachers were directed to pair this reinforcement with the school's expectation of "work hard." The school-level tier 1 team set a goal to reduce the daily ODR rate to two ODRs per day for the subsequent month. The team then shared the school-wide data and the action steps to implement the increased reinforcement to all faculty and provided them with an increased supply of PBIS tickets.

When the team met the following month to review data, they found that the rate of ODRs had decreased, but only to ten ODRs per day; they did not achieve their goal. The team decided that a review of other data sources may help better identify the problem with precision and generate more effective solutions to address the identified problem. The team then reviewed trends from the recently completed winter reading screenings. The results reflected students were not maintaining their beginning of year proficiency status. In fact, they were losing ground with many students who were at benchmark at the beginning of the year now scoring in the below benchmark range. Across grade levels, approximately 40% to 50% of students were meeting benchmark status on the reading screening. The data analyst had prepared data summaries for the team to review and was able to drill down and find that many of the ODRs were happening during reading instruction. The team determined that improving reading instruction to more effectively help students improve reading skills was a necessary action step. The North Side team recognized that the guided reading groups currently being implemented, requiring students to guess when presented with unknown words and use picture clues in leveled texts, was not effective. In fact, the team recognized this approach was detrimental to students' reading skill development, as evidenced by decreases in percentages of students remaining at benchmark from the beginning of the year, with increases in percentages of students scoring in the below benchmark to well below benchmark ranges. The team generated a new solution action to address the concerns reflected in high ODRs from the classroom that included explicit, systematic instruction grounded in the science of reading and the use of decodable texts instead of leveled texts during small group reading activities.

Early Warning System data (EWS) can help schools determine when students are off-track for graduation, at an increased level of risk for dropping out of high school, and are less likely to attend college (Balfanz et al., 2014). Key metrics for attendance, behavior, and course performance, known as the "A-B-Cs" have been identified to let school teams know when specific students are at risk. There are identified thresholds for each of these research-based predictors of student engagement. Students who have attended less than 90% of school, have one office discipline referral or suspension for behavior, and have failed one major course (e.g., mathematics, English language arts) are significantly less likely to graduate without intervention. When schools adopt an EWS, PBIS data (i.e., ODRs) are viewed in tandem with attendance and course performance data, helping teams identify students in need of intervention to help them stay on track for graduation. Similar to reviewing and analyzing other data sources (i.e., ODR, academic data), teams must ask if specific groups of students are represented more than others when flagged as being at-risk in an EWS. Resources to learn more about supporting research and value of an EWS can be found from the Everyone Graduates Center at Johns Hopkins University https://new.every1graduates.org/.

Special Education Data

Special education data provide a wealth of information about equitable practices. Teams can investigate risk indices and risk ratios to determine if groups of students are disproportionately represented in special education overall or within a particular disability category. Data can help teams ask meaningful and deep questions about systems that contribute to overrepresentation. For example, in a school district with a small population of English learners, are English learners disproportionately identified as students with specific learning disabilities in reading and writing? Are specific groups of students at higher risk for manifestation determination processes due to repeated exclusionary discipline practices? How are students referred for evaluations for special education? What do identification processes look like? When standardized, norm-referenced assessments are included as part of a comprehensive evaluation, consider if those tests have been normed on the population of students for which they are being used to aid in the evaluation process. Are specific groups of students more likely to be placed in more restrictive programming (e.g., full-time emotional support) than other groups?

Gifted Education Eligibility and Enrollment

Likewise, teams can analyze data on referral and identification rates for enrollment in these gifted and talented programs. Decades of research consistently document that students of color, particularly students who identify as Black and Latinx, are underrepresented in gifted and talented programming (e.g., Erwin & Worrell, 2012; Ford et al., 2008; Grissom & Redding, 2016). Teams can look at the demographics of students receiving gifted education and attend to any trends in the data suggesting disproportionate identification and/or placement rates. Are groups of students underrepresented in gifted and talented programs? If so, what groups of students? Might cultural differences or English language proficiency be masking gifted abilities? Again, teams should think about the systems, including aspects of the system (e.g., referral process; identification process) that may impact student opportunity to participate in gifted and talented programs.

Scenario

Red Oak Elementary School, located within a large urban school district, serves students from kindergarten through 3rd grade. The student population at Red Oak Elementary School is comprised of 75% Latinx, 20% Black, and 5% White students. Of the approximately 400 students enrolled in the school, there are no students in the entire building who are eligible for gifted programming. A newly hired administrator who oversees student services quickly recognizes the problem of no students identified as gifted. When meeting with the building leadership team, she asks for details on the referral and identification process for eligibility and access to gifted programming. The team reports that teachers can refer any student they suspect of potential giftedness for a screening, and the school counselor then administers a brief, individually administered IQ test to that student. If the student scores 130 (98th percentile) or higher, then that student would be referred for a comprehensive evaluation to determine eligibility for gifted education. Team members explain this has been their process for years; however, their students never score 130 or higher so gifted evaluations are just not ever recommended at their building. The student services director and the team engage in self-reflection as well as reflect on the referral system employed. They review research on best practices in assessment for suspected giftedness. They learn and come to an agreement that a comprehensive approach, including information drawn from a wide variety of sources relevant to a student's area(s) of suspected giftedness, is necessary, and that the use of a single brief IQ measure is insufficient for identifying students for gifted programming, especially students from minoritized groups.

Educational and Extracurricular Opportunities

Enrollment data for advanced placement courses and extracurricular opportunities can shed light on access for academic opportunity. Take for example, students' opportunities to enroll in advanced-level courses to be well prepared for college and future careers or even the opportunity to take college-in-high school courses to earn credits toward a college degree while in high school. Teams must consider data for groups of students participating in advanced courses in mathematics, English language arts, the sciences, technology and more, as research indicates disparities in opportunity and access exist for minoritized groups (Klopfenstein, 2004; Ream & Rumberger, 2008; Xu et al., 2021). Are there specific groups of students enrolled in advanced courses at a disproportionate rate than other student groups? Teams, again, must consider the systematic processes for determining which students receive access to these educational opportunities. In a similar vein, school teams should consider reviewing data regarding participation in extracurricular opportunities such as clubs, student leadership positions, and sports to determine if all student groups have equitable access. For example, do English learners have the opportunity to enroll in advanced placement courses? Are students with disabilities provided with opportunities to access extracurricular opportunities? Data from enrollment and participation in advanced educational as well as extracurricular opportunities can help teams answer these questions.

Mental Health and Behavioral Data

A number of instruments exist to help school teams screen for students who may be at-risk for social, emotional, behavioral, and mental health concerns. Universal screeners are typically brief and are administered for all students. Data from universal screening instruments can be used in tiered systems of support to identify students who may require advanced supports in addition to tier 1 as well as match supports to identified student need. It is important for school teams to recognize their ethical obligation to intervene once needs are identified with screening data.

Open-access sites and resources are available to help school teams compare universal screening tools. Romer and colleagues (2020) provide a comprehensive guide teams can review to assist with prerequisite information to consider prior to screening, including selection of a universal social, emotional, and behavioral (SEB) screening instrument, as well as legal and ethical considerations. Of key importance is that universal SEB screening as a process must be grounded in sound procedures for implementing evidence-based screeners to ensure school teams access technically adequate data to inform decisions within a system aiming to improve mental wellness, prevent SEB problems, and ensure all students have access to a continuum of SEB supports (Romer et al., 2020).

Keeping equity at the forefront of SEB screening is essential. Teams must consider many factors to ensure that screening instruments accurately and equitably identify students who have SEB needs, and that resources are effectively aligned and allocated for every student identified with SEB needs. Teams will want to ask a variety of questions as they explore, install, and implement an SEB screener. First, teams will want to ask is this a fair screening instrument. In other words, does this measure perform similarly across student subgroups, including groups defined by gender, race/ethnicity, language, geographic region, and sexual orientation (Romer et al., 2020)? Are risk decisions proportionate across student subgroups? How often will data be disaggregated and analyzed for different subgroups (e.g., gender, ethnicity, IEP status, etc.)? Are any subgroups overrepresented or underrepresented from screening results as having SEB needs? Are evidence-based interventions in place to support needs identified on the SEB screening? Are all students identified as having SEB needs receiving intervention that are aligned to their specific needs?

There are several open-access online sites teams can investigate as they explore SEB screening instruments. The University of Missouri's Evidence-Based Intervention Network (2022) provides technical briefs highlighting psychometric adequacy, administration and scoring steps, and other key information on several SEB screening measures including the Student Risk Screening Scale (SRSS; Drummond, 1994) and the Social, Academic, and Emotional Behavior Risk Screener (SAEBRS; Kilgus et al., 2013). All briefs can be accessed online at the University of Missouri's Evidence-Based Intervention site: https://education. missouri.edu/ebi/category/behavior-assessments-screening/ (2022). The National Center on Intensive Intervention provides a source for tools charts where educators, families, and other stakeholders can review independently established criteria on the technical adequacy of SEB screeners at https://charts.intensiveintervention.org/bscreening, as well as other screeners and interventions.

When students are identified as having a need for additional strategic or intensive social, emotional, or behavioral support, data should drive decision making. First, looking at percentages of students receiving advanced tiers of behavioral supports is essential to resource allocation and ensuring that the resources needed are available to support identified student needs. For example, if 50% of students in a school have three or more ODRs and are identified as being at-risk on a SEB screener, efforts need to be focused on strengthening tier 1 efforts. Schools typically do not have the resources to provide strategic and individualized intervention to 50% of the student population. These data would also indicate that tier 1 supports are not effective with regard to meeting the majority of students' needs. Likewise, when tier 1 is strong, this helps enhance the efficacy of interventions at tiers 2 and 3, as a number of interventions build upon tier 1 in frequency, focus, and intensity. Additionally, teams must determine which students are identified as needing advanced tiers of supports. Are certain subgroups represented more than others? If so, teams need to dig deeper to determine what systemic factors may be contributing to disproportionality.

Out-of-school placement data for behavioral or mental health reasons are an important data source not to be overlooked. Teams should determine if there are students in their school being placed into alternative education settings due to behavioral concerns. If so, are certain groups of students placed into alternative education at disproportionate rates when compared to other groups of students? Teams must reflect upon systems that may be contributing to enrolling students to alternative education programs. Even when programs are not physically outside of the home school, are there students who are enrolled in an alternative education program on-site at the school? What students are being placed in those in-house programs, and are there aspects of systems contributing to those placements? How long are students enrolled in alternative programs? Are students experiencing successful outcomes as a result of being placed in that program (e.g., academically, socially, behaviorally)?

Scenario

Meadow Area School District is a large, urban school district. To save costs, the district established its own in-district alternative education program for students with behavioral concerns in grades 7–12. The program, called Steps to Success, is housed in its own building, which is separate from all the other district school buildings. The classrooms in the building are crowded and at full capacity. Students at the Steps to Success school do not have access to the same instructional programs or activities as students enrolled in other district schools. In the state where Meadow Area School District is located, approximately 16% of students statewide are identified with a disability and have an IEP. In the Meadow Area School District, approximately 17.2% of students are identified with a disability and have an IEP. However, approximately 55% of students enrolled at the Steps to Success school are identified with disabilities and have IEPs. Additionally, less than 30% of students who are placed at Steps to Success ever return to their neighborhood school where they access the district's general education curriculum. Parents of a 9th grade student who was unilaterally placed in the Steps to Success program after being involved in a fight at his high school noticed their son's performance started to decline after being placed at the alternative school. The parents expressed concern to administrators that their son, a student with mental health challenges and an IEP for emotional support services, was earning lower grades and receiving frequent discipline referrals in this program. The administrators at the program shared they use a point system and that when students violate school rules they are assigned points as a consequence. As students accumulate points, they lose privileges (i.e., the more points they have, the more privileges they lose). The administrator could not describe any supports for all students that included explicit teaching of expectations, reinforcement for displaying expected behaviors, or any social-emotional learning (SEL) curriculum to help students develop essential skills for success. The student's parents filed a complaint with the state department of education's special education dispute hotline and were able to find support through a volunteer organization providing educational advocacy services for students with disabilities. The parents' advocacy efforts served as a catalyst for systemic change to make improvements in the district for students with disabilities.

Another valuable source of information for teams to access is data on referrals to community mental health services and school-based mental health supports. Evaluating trends for referrals to mental health supports and services can provide insights on which students are eligible for and accessing these supports. Data may also show potential barriers for access. For example, rural areas may not have the mental health resources in close proximity to schools and as a result, few students are able to access those supports. In urban and suburban areas, long wait lists may be barriers to access. Insurance requirements may be barriers for many students, regardless of geographic location. Likewise, school psychologists, school counselors, and school social workers may be working within high student-to-staff ratios in the school setting and lack the capacity to provide needed school-based mental health supports. For example, one study found that when school psychologists worked in a ratio of 700:1 or less (700 students to one school psychologist), they were able to spend significantly more time providing mental health supports to students (Eklund et al., 2017). Evaluating data for access and problem-solving around barriers to services are necessary steps in ensuring students in need of mental health supports receive those supports.

Prevention and mitigation of adverse psychological impact of traumatic events through adoption of a comprehensive crisis prevention and intervention model, such as the National Association of School Psychologists' PREPaRE (Brock et al., 2016), integrates very well with PBIS structure. When there is a reinforced sense of shared ownership and pride physically visible in a school community (e.g., PBIS displays in the school environment), students and staff members feel more confident to intervene and challenge inappropriate behavior when it occurs (Scheider et al., 2000). Teams can analyze school-level data with regard to the number of crisis responses documented by student services personnel (e.g., school counselors, school social workers, school psychologists) and administrators to ascertain information regarding social, emotional, and mental wellness. Additionally, analyzing data regarding the number and types of threat assessments conducted, students involved, and outcomes may be a data source that is overlooked but highly important. Teams can ask questions as they review these data such as: Are there groups of students involved in crisis situations more than others? Are there aspects of systems that are contributing to crisis or threat situations for specific groups of students more than others? Are there trends in the data when crises occur more often? What outcomes are associated with crises and threats? Analyzing data around crisis intervention and threat assessment can help teams improve crisis prevention and response efforts.

Perception Data

Perception data provide teams with meaningful and valuable information to inform implementation efforts. Perception data can help teams better understand what students, families, community partners, and faculty and staff think about the school climate and environment. Do students feel safe and supported at school? Do families and community partners report positive relationships with school staff? Do faculty and staff perceive the school to be a positive work environment? Data from climate surveys can be used to drive action planning to improve school climate. While aggregate data are helpful, having the ability to disaggregate data for minoritized and marginalized groups can help teams determine if all groups perceive the school to be inclusive and foster feelings of safety and belonging.

Student Voice

Students are the center of educational efforts. Student perception of the school environment is essential in informing PBIS. Comparing student perception data with adult perception data can help PBIS implementation teams find common themes of agreement and areas where there is disconnect. Student perception data can provide valuable insight into areas where adults may have blind spots. For example, the Center on PBIS (2022) has an English and Spanish *School Climate Survey* that is free for school systems to use, including student surveys for students grades 3 to 12. On the *School Climate Survey: Elementary* for students in grades 3–6, students are asked to rate 11 positively stated items (e.g., "*I like school,*" "*I feel safe at school,*" "*Teachers treat me with respect*") using a Likert scale with response options ranging from *never* to *always* (Center on PBIS, 2022). The *School Climate Survey: Middle/High* for students in grades 7–12 is similar to the elementary version; however, it includes two versions: brief, which is similar to the elementary version (nine items), and extended (36 items). Students rate each item using a 4-point Likert scale with ratings ranging from *strongly agree* to *strongly disagree*. The surveys are anonymous and can be administered paper/pencil or online from the PBIS Applications website www.pbisapps.org. It is recommended the surveys be completed twice per year (fall and spring).

The *School Climate Survey* provides teams with insight into how students feel about school and their experiences in the school. Data can be analyzed and linked to action steps by PBIS teams to create an environment where all students want to be present and belong. For example, if there are groups of students who indicate they do not feel safe at school, teams would want to reflect upon systems, policies, and practices that may be contributing to this perception. Survey data can also help teams generate additional questions. Take for instance, in a building of grades 6–8, if 6th graders are the group reporting they disagree or strongly disagree with feeling safe at school, additional information and data may be needed to help identify the root cause of the problem and identify and implement an action plan. The student team could be engaged in the problem-solving process and provide valuable insight. For example, the student team may recognize that the 6th grade hallway is not well monitored during class transitions and that there are groups of students who are teasing other students about social media video posts during these transitions. Using the problem-solving process, action steps can be generated to most effectively address the issue.

School Personnel Perceptions

The Center on PBIS (2022) includes a *School Climate Survey: School Personnel* component. This survey is designed to be administered to all personnel working in a school. Staff complete this 29-item survey measuring areas of staff connectedness, structure for learning, safety, peer/adult relations, physical environment, and parental involvement. Data can be disaggregated by staff type: administrative, teaching, certificated, and classified. Items regarding demographic data are also included, with options of *prefer not to answer* for additional analysis. School personnel rate each item using a 4-point Likert scale with ratings ranging from *strongly agree* to *strongly disagree*. Teams can use results to inform drive action planning. Are there areas where school personnel hold negative perceptions. For example, if the data reflect most staff report they disagree or strongly disagree with the statement, "Teachers at my school frequently recognize students for good behavior," this can be directly addressed in the team's action planning. Teams can look at proximal data (e.g., monthly data on PBIS acknowledgments) and distal data (the next administration of the *School Climate Survey: School Personnel* version) to determine the degree of efficacy of their action planning.

Family and Community Perceptions

The Center on PBIS (2022) also has a *School Climate Survey: Family* that schools can provide to families for anonymous completion in either English or Spanish. Similar to the *School Climate Survey: Elementary* and *School Climate Survey: Middle/High*, the family version includes optional demographic items, including if their student receives special education, gifted education, or participates in advanced placement courses. Families are provided with 21 positively stated items embedded within five areas related to school climate including teaching and learning, school safety, interpersonal relationships, instructional environment, and parent involvement. Caregivers indicate their ratings on a 4-point

Likert scale with ratings ranging from *strongly agree* to *strongly disagree* (Center on PBIS, 2022). PBIS teams can use data from the *School Climate Survey* as a starting point to see how families feel when they are in the school, their perceptions of the school environment and opportunities for their children, and their relationships with school personnel. PBIS teams can engage their family representatives in the problem-solving process around identified areas of need and develop solutions to address those needs.

Additional Resources

The *Comprehensive School Climate Inventory* (CSCI) from the National School Climate Center (NSCC) at https://schoolclimate.org/services/measuring-school-climate-csci/ is another school climate survey that provides a profile of a school community's particular strengths and areas in need of improvement. Similar to the *School Climate Survey* (2022), schools can use the CSCI to assess student, parent/guardian, and school personnel perceptions to inform decision making. The NSCC CSCI can support school systems with continuous improvement and shared leadership across the district, school building, classroom, student, and community domains through an action planning process to inform policy, procedure, and practice. For example, at the district-level, information from the CSCI can be used to develop school climate-informed policies that focus on strong relationships within the school to prevent potential issues and help adults effectively respond if issues arise. At the community level, information obtained from the CSCI can inform action planning to strengthen relationships within the school between students, staff, and parents, as well as the school's relationships with the broader community, such as local businesses and civic organizations (National School Climate Center, 2021). This provides a great opportunity for PBIS teams to engage team members from various stakeholders groups (school personnel, families, students, community representatives) to participate in the problem-solving process with regard to specific concerns reflected in the CSCI data.

There are a number of open-access resources available to help teams strengthen efforts to build stronger relationships with students, families, school personnel, and community partners in light of results obtained on various climate surveys measuring perception data. The Center on PBIS provides a helpful brief (La Salle, 2022) describing how schools can use the results from the parent and school personnel *School Climate Survey* (Center on PBIS, 2022) to inform action planning. The National Parent Teacher Association (PTA, 2008) provides national standards and an implementation guide for best practices in family-school partnerships and includes a comprehensive action planning resource that can be found on their website www.pta.org/home/run-your-pta/National-Standards-for-Family-School-Partnerships. An open-access technical brief from the University of Connecticut Collaboratory on School and Child Health (Iovino et al., 2022) found at https://csch.uconn.edu/wp-content/uploads/sites/2206/2022/01/CSCH-Brief-Resources-to-Support-Family-School-Engagement.pdf provides a curated repository of resources to support meaningful family engagement that teams can investigate to strengthen their efforts and identify evidence-based practices to link to action planning. State departments of education may have their own repositories of resources as well. For example, the Pennsylvania Department of Education has developed an open-access *Staff and Student Wellness Guide* (2020) available online or as a PDF to help schools support staff and student wellness with actionable items school teams can implement. It can be found at www.education.pa.gov/Schools/safeschools/emergencyplanning/COVID-19/School ReopeningGuidance/ReopeningPreKto12/CreatingEquitableSchool Systems/Pages/Support-Social-and-Emotional-Wellness.aspx.

Summary

Beginning the journey to comprehensive and fidelity implementation of PBIS includes establishing teaming structures necessary for implementation, effective frameworks for team problem-solving, and audits of self and system awareness. Data are essential in guiding infrastructure development and initial installation as well as ongoing problem-solving and decision making. While aggregate data provide a first step for teams to look at the big picture of systems, aggregate data are not enough to ensure systems are working for every student. Teams must have the skills to disaggregate data to determine if systems are effective for not only the student body as a whole, but also for minoritized and marginalized student groups. The following chapter will describe implementation and evaluation with fidelity. These core underpinnings provide the foundation to build and embed equitable practices to sustain positive outcomes. We'll see you at the next stop on our journey!

Chapter 2: Seeds for Growth

- ◆ The SWPBIS journey begins with teams. Essential teaming structures include a **district-level team**, **school-level team (tier 1)**, **student-led team (tier 1)**, **advanced tiers team**, and **individual student problem-solving team**.
- ◆ A **validated framework (i.e., Team-Initiated Problem Solving; TIPS) for team meeting facilitation** to include problem-solving, roles and responsibilities, and team meeting minutes is needed to help teams analyze data for decision making.
- ◆ **Systems awareness** and **self-awareness** help collective teams and individual team members begin their journey and focus on problem-solving with an equitable mindset.
- ◆ **Data sources** including disciplinary data (ODRs, suspensions, expulsions), academic data, early warning system data, special education data, behavioral data, crisis and threat assessment data, mental health data, and perception data provide teams with a **view of their systems**.
- ◆ While data from these sources help teams see a global picture, **disaggregating data by marginalized/minoritized groups provides valuable information to help teams determine whether and where problems may rest**.

Vignette/Example

Distributed leadership, operationally defined roles and responsibilities for each team member, as well as pre-planned, dedicated time for the leadership team to meet, plan, and problem-solve around data helps not only with infrastructure development and initial installation but also with sustainability of PBIS (e.g., McIntosh et al., 2013). This scenario illustrates how teams can begin the journey of building, implementing, and sustaining PBIS to create equitable practices and grow a positive school climate.

The Elk Creek Middle-High School (not a real school name) is a combined 7–12 building in a rural area with limited resources. The principal, school psychologist, and special education director observed many students, especially students with disabilities, were being referred to the office for discipline at seemingly high rates. These three individuals compiled school-wide ODR data for analysis and soon realized that nearly 40% of all students in the school of approximately 500 students had been referred to the office for at least one disciplinary infraction (i.e., 200 students had one or more office referrals). Upon further investigation of the data, it became evident that 25% of all students had been referred to the office for discipline two or more times (approximately 125 students), and 15% of students had four or more referrals (approximately 75 students), with some students having as many as 20 referrals by December. When analyzing ODR data for the 85 students enrolled at Elk Creek MS-HS identified with disabilities, the trio discovered 78 out of the 85 students with disabilities (92%) had at least one ODR by December, and the students with the highest numbers of referrals in the building were all students identified with emotional and behavioral disabilities. Upon further investigation, 90% of the students with emotional and behavioral disabilities received at least three or more days of suspension. The trio recognized there were systemic issues that needed to be addressed. They decided to explore the possibility of installing PBIS. Their first step was reviewing the resources on the Center on PBIS website, www.pbis.org/pbis/getting-started, and they were excited to learn that every state in the United States has a team to help by providing training, coaching, and technical assistance. They were able to get connected with an external coach who could provide support to Elk Creek. The team recognized that based on preliminary data of high ODRs, one of their challenges would be to help staff recognize the misconception that disciplinary exclusion (i.e., suspension) is not an intervention that has a positive impact upon changing student behavior and that, in fact, it is a practice that is harmful and further disengages students from school.

Their next step was to form a leadership team of eight members. They knew it would be important to include voice and perspective from various stakeholders representative of the Elk Creek school community. The team allocated periods of time across a year for infrastructure building and planning, and each member had an assigned role with a set of responsibilities. The team began working with their external coach to learn about research-based components of SWPBIS and how to apply those components in the context of their school environment. One of the first orders of business was to complete an initial audit with a goal of equitable outcomes for every student. While the initial trio of the principal, special education director, and school psychologist focused solely on ODR data, there were other sources of data and information on which to capitalize. The team also looked at academic data, mental health screening data, special education data, out-of-school placement data, and school climate data. They investigated existing systems including school and community support and practices (e.g., policies, procedures, memoranda of understanding). They recognized systems' strengths, as well as areas for improvement. An area of strength was a strong partnership with a community mental health provider that provided a seamless process for any student to receive free access to mental health supports. Baseline surveys assessing staff and community perceptions of the school and surrounding community's perceptions of protection and risk factors were administered (*School Climate Survey*; Center on PBIS, 2022). The team also completed a baseline measure of staff perception of features of PBIS already in place. By working with their state technical assistance provider, the team had support with regard to training, technical assistance, accessing PBISApps resources, and ongoing coaching.

The school leadership team created a shared online drive (e.g., Google Drive) where all team members were able to collaborate on the development of a PBIS manual and necessary supplementary materials that would be used and shared with all staff to communicate common vision, language, and practices to aid in PBIS implementation. Systems, data, and practices were at the heart of all the team's work.

Next, a team of 12 students, two students from each grade level, representative of the school's population, was installed as the new student team to work in tandem with the adult SWPBIS building team as they developed infrastructure necessary to implement PBIS. The student team designed their own brief survey, with support of the adult school leadership team, to solicit input from all students in the school regarding desired acknowledgments and their perceptions of strengths and needs of the school culture. The adult and student teams worked together to establish school-wide expectations in positively stated terms and student-friendly language. They developed lessons and videos to teach expected behaviors to all students, as well as a system to include meaningful acknowledgments for students and staff. Problem behaviors were operationally defined into mutually exclusive categories and classified as either major (i.e., office referral) and minor (i.e., teacher-managed). Throughout the development of infrastructure components, faculty and staff on the team were provided with updates and opportunities to provide feedback to establish buy-in and contextual fit. The school-level adult and student team planned kickoff sessions, first rolling out to faculty and staff, then to the entire student population with faculty and staff supporting. They planned a high-energy kickoff for the students, including music, acknowledgments, and introduction to SWPBIS in their school.

After initial kickoff and implementation, the teams began monthly meetings using the TIPS process to analyze data, set goals for improvement and monitor progress, and engage in systems-level problem solving. They learned how to calculate risk indices and risk ratios to determine if disproportionate outcomes were occurring for any student group, including students with disabilities, and included these data in their problem-solving process. The team recognized the need to get a strong tier 1 in place to reduce ODRs and more effectively support every student; however, they knew their journey could not stop with only tier 1 support in place. The team's next steps are to continue implementation and refinement of tier 1 and to develop necessary infrastructure to support tier 2 and tier 3.

Reference List

Balfanz, R., Byrnes, V., & Fox, J. (2014). Sent home and put off-track: The antecedents, disproportionalities, and consequences of being suspended in the ninth grade. *Journal of Applied Research on Children: Informing Policy for Children at Risk, 5*(2), Article 13.

Brock, S. E., Nickerson, A. B., Louvar Reeves, M. A., Conolly, C. N., Jimerson, S. R., Pesce, R. C., & Lazzaro, B. R. (2016). *School crisis prevention and intervention: The PREPaRE model* (2nd ed.). National Association of School Psychologists.

Bullis, M., & Yovanoff, P. (2006). Idle hands: Community employment experiences of formerly incarcerated youth. *Journal of Emotional and Behavioral Disorders, 14,* 71–85.

Center on PBIS. (2022, January). *School climate survey (SCS) suite manual.* University of Oregon. www.pbis.org

Drummond, T. (1994). *The student risk screening scale (SRSS).* Josephine County Mental Health Program.

Eklund, K., Meyer, L., Way, S., & Mclean, D. (2017). School psychologists as mental health providers: The impact of staffing ratios and Medicaid on service provisions. *Psychology in the Schools, 54,* 279–293. https://doi.org/10.1002/pits.21996

Erwin, J. O., & Worrell, F. C. (2012). Assessment practices and the under-representation of minority students in gifted and talented education. *Journal of Psychoeducational Assessment, 30*(1), 74–87. https://doi.org/10.1177/0734282911428197

Ford, D. Y., Grantham, T. C., & Whiting, G. W. (2008). Culturally and linguistically diverse students in gifted education: Recruitment and retention issues. *Exceptional Children, 74*(3), 289–306.

Grissom, J. A., & Redding, C. (2016). *Discretion and disproportionality: Explaining the under-representation of high-achieving students of color in gifted programs.* AERA Open.

Heidelberg, K., Rutherford, L., & Parks, T. W. (2022). A preliminary analysis assessing SWPBIS implementation fidelity in relation to disciplinary outcomes of Black students in urban schools. *The Urban Review, 54*(1), 138–154.

Horner, R. H., Newton, J. S., Todd, A. W., Algozzine, B., Algozzine, K., Cusumano, D. L., & Preston, A. I. (2015). *The team-initiated problem solving (TIPS II) training materials.* www.TIPS2info.blogspot.com

Hughes, C., & Dexter, D. D. (2022). *Universal screening within a response-to-intervention model.* National Center on Learning Disabilities: RTI Action Network. Retrieved May 14, 2022, from www.rtinetwork.org/learn/research/universal-screening-within-a-rti-model

Iovino, E. A., Koslouski, J. B., Chafouleas, S. M., & Perry, H. Y. (2022). *Resources to support family-school engagement.* UConn Collaboratory on School and Child Health. http://csch.uconn.edu/

Kilgus, S. P., Chafouleas, S. M., & Riley-Tillman, T. C. (2013). Development and initial validation of the social and academic behavior risk screener for elementary grades. *School Psychology Quarterly, 28,* 210–226.

Klopfenstein, K. (2004). Advanced placement: Do minorities have equal opportunity? *Economics of Education Review, 23*(2), 115–131.

La Salle, T. P. (2022, January). *How are schools using the parent and personnel school climate surveys?* Center on PBIS, University of Oregon. www.pbis.org

Lee, T., Cornell, D., Gregory, A., & Xitao, F. (2011). High suspension schools and dropout rates for black and white students, *Education & Treatment of Children, 34(2),* (pp. 167–192). https://doi.org/10.1353/etc.2011.0014

McIntosh, K., Campbell, A. L., Russell Carter, D., & Zumbo, B. (2009). Concurrent validity of office discipline referrals and cut points used in schoolwide positive behavior support. *Behavioral Disorders, 34*(2), 100–113.

McIntosh, K., Frank, J. L., & Spaulding, S. A. (2010). Establishing research-based trajectories of office discipline referrals for individual students. *School Psychology Review, 39*(3), 380–394.

McIntosh, K., & Goodman, S. (2016). *Integrated multi-tiered system of support: Blending RTI and PBIS.* Guilford.

McIntosh, K., Horner, R. H., Chard, D. J., Boland. B., & Good, R. H. (2006). The use of reading and behavior screening measures to predict non-response to school wide positive behavior support: A longitudinal analysis. *School Psychology Review, 35,* 275–291.

McIntosh, K., Mercer, S. H., Hume, A. E., Frank, J. L., Turri, M. G., & Matthews, S. (2013). Factors related to sustained implementation of school-wide positive behavior support. *Exceptional Children, 79,* 293–311.

National Center on Intensive Intervention at American Institutes for Research. (2021). *Academic screening tools chart.* https://charts. intensiveintervention.org/ascreening?_ga=2.245417028.17659 38025.1659966855-815631209.1659966855

National Parent Teacher Association. (2008). *National standards for family-school partnerships: An implementation guide.* www.pta.org/home/ run-your-pta/National-Standards-for-Family-School-Partnerships

National School Climate Center. (2021). *Measuring school climate: CSCI.* https://schoolclimate.org/services/measuring-school-climate-csci/

O'Malley, M., Voight, A., & Izu, J. (2014). Engaging students in school climate improvement: A student voice strategy. In M. J. Furlong, R. Gilman, & E. S. Huebner (Eds.). *Handbook of positive psychology in schools* (pp. 329–346). Routledge.

Paine, S., & Paine, C. K. (2002). Promoting safety and success in school by developing students' strengths. In M. R. Shinn, G. Stoner, & H. M. Walker (Eds.), *Interventions for academic and behavior problems: Preventive and remedial approaches* (pp. 89–108). National Association of School Psychologists.

Payno-Simmons, R. L. (2021). Centering equity in school discipline: The Michigan PBIS equity pilot. *Preventing School Failure: Alternative Education for Children and Youth, 65*(4), 343–353. doi:10.1080/10 45988X.2021.1937024

Pennsylvania Department of Education. (2020). *Staff and student wellness guide creating equitable school systems: A roadmap for education leaders—2020–2021.* Pennsylvania Department of Education.

Pinkelman, S. E., McIntosh, K., Rasplica, C. K., Berg, T., & Strickland-Cohen, M. K. (2018). Perceived enablers and barriers related to sustainability of school-wide positive behavioral interventions and supports. *Behavioral Disorders, 40*(3), 171–183.

Ream, R. K., & Rumberger, R. W. (2008). Student engagement, peer social capital, and school dropout among Mexican American and non-Latino White students. *Sociology of Education, 81*(2), 109–139.

Romer, N., von der Embse, N., Eklund, K., Kilgus, S., Perales, K., Splett, J. W., Sudlo, S., & Wheeler, D. (2020). *Best practices in social, emotional, and behavioral screening: An implementation guide.* Version 2.0. https://smhcollaborative.org/universalscreening/

Scheider, T., Walker, H., & Sprague, J. (2000). *Safe school design: A handbook for educational leaders applying the principles of crime prevention through environmental design.* ERIC Clearinghouse on Educational Management. https://eric.ed.gov/?id=ED449541

School-Wide Information System. (2019). *SWIS summary.* Educational and Community Supports. pbisapps.org.

Skiba, R. J., Horner, R. H., Chung, C., Rausch, M. K., May, S. L., & Tobin, T. (2011). Race is not neutral: A national investigation of African American and Latino disproportionality in school discipline. *School Psychology Review, 40*(1), 85–107.

Sugai, G. (2010). *Working smarter matrix: Committee/group self-assessment and action planning.* Retrieved May 14, 2022, from https://nemtss.unl.edu/wp-content/uploads/2018/08/PBIS-Working-Smarter-Matrix.pdf

Sugai, G., Sprague, J. R., Horner, R. H., & Walker, H. M. (2000). Preventing school violence: The use of office discipline referrals to assess and monitor school-wide discipline interventions. *Journal of Emotional and Behavioral Disorders, 8*(2), 94–101. doi:10.1177/106342660000800205

University of Missouri: Evidence-Based Intervention Network. (2022). *Category- behavior assessments: Screening.* https://education.missouri.edu/ebi/category/behavior-assessments-screening/

Xu, D., Solanki, S., & Fink, J. (2021). College acceleration for all? Mapping racial gaps in advanced placement and dual enrollment participation. *American Educational Research Journal, 58*(5), 954–992.

Checklist for Considerations for PBIS Team Membership

This checklist can be used to assist with decision-making regarding teaming structures when membership for each team is being established or reviewed (e.g., annual action planning, changes in personnel).

☐ **District-Level Team**
  o District-level administrator(s)
  o Building-level administrators
  o Building-level coach/coordinator from school-level team(s)
  o Student representatives
  o Family representatives
  o Community representatives
  o Other district-level representatives: _____

☐ **School-Level PBIS Tier 1 Team**
  o Administrator
  o Individual with expertise in behavior and mental health (e.g., school psychologist, school social worker, BCBA, school counselor, behavioral specialist)
  o Individual(s) with instructional expertise
  o Individuals with specialized expertise (e.g., speech-language pathologist)
  o Paraeducators, support staff representative(s)
  o Family representative(s)
  o Community representative(s)
  o Student voice/representative(s)
  o Other representative(s): _____

☐ **Grade-Level or Department-Level Teams**
  o Grade-level or department-level, dependent upon structure of school
  o All teachers for a specific grade level (e.g., 2nd grade in elementary school) or for an entire department (e.g., math department in a high school)

- o Administrator
- o Other team member(s): _____

- [ ] **Student School-Level PBIS Leadership Team**
  - o Student members representative of the school population, including representation across all:
    - o Grade levels
    - o Social groups
    - o Extracurricular activities (e.g., music, athletics, arts)
    - o Areas of academic focus (e.g., career and technical studies)
    - o Demographic groups
    - o Other considerations for representative membership:
      _____

- [ ] **Advanced Tiers Team**
  - o Individual with expertise in behavior and mental health (e.g., school psychologist, school social worker, BCBA, school counselor)
  - o Administrator
  - o Special education teacher(s)
  - o Content specialists
  - o Support personnel
  - o Other team member(s): _____

- [ ] **Individual Student Problem-Solving Team (Membership for Each Student's Team is Customized Based Upon Student's Strengths and Needs)**
  - o Family/caregivers
  - o Student, when appropriate
  - o Teacher(s)
  - o Administrator
  - o Content specialist (e.g., reading specialist, ESL teacher)
  - o Related service provider (e.g., speech and language pathologist)
  - o Other team member(s): _____

Checklist for Considerations for Establishing and Sustaining a Student PBIS Leadership Team

☐ **Establishing Infrastructure**
- o Ensure administrative and faculty support for a student team is in place
  - o Ensure faculty or staff member(s) can serve in an advisory role with time allocated in their schedule
  - o Ensure an administrative representative is able to meet with faculty advisor and student team at least monthly to support any administrative decision-making needed
- o Ensure there is common, pre-planned time for students to meet, at least monthly, with administrative and faculty advisor support
  - o Examples may include common homeroom time, scheduled elective period, or scheduled club time

☐ **Team Selection**
- o Determine procedures for equitably selecting student representatives to serve on the SWPBIS student leadership team
- o Is the student team representative of the student population?
- o Establish procedures for how students are notified of their selection to be SWPBIS student team representatives
  - o Examples may include sending formal congratulations letters home or inviting students to an informational meeting
- o Provide the new student team with orientation to research-based components of SWPBIS and how those components apply to their school and to their roles as members of the student leadership team

☐ **Team Operating Procedures**
- o Roles are established, and student team leadership is distributed

- ○ Meetings are scheduled at least monthly
- ○ Students have access to school-level data necessary for problem-solving (e.g., attendance trends, school-wide climate data, office discipline referral school-wide trends)
- ○ A meeting protocol (e.g., Team-Initiated Problem Solving) is used to ensure decisions are based on student input, data, and needs; the meeting protocol includes an action plan
- ○ Administrative support is provided

□ **Implementation of Student Team Decisions**
- ○ Adult support is provided to ensure administrative items on the action plan are implemented
- ○ Students implement student-led actions

□ **Sustainability**
- ○ Ensure procedures are in place to replace members who graduate, move, etc.
- ○ Ensure procedures are in place for adult support (faculty advisor and systems support from administration)
- ○ Orientation for new team members is provided when they join the team

Checklist for Potential Data Sources to Analyze for Potential Disproportionality and Problem-Solving

□ **Office Discipline Referral (ODR) Data**
- ○ Office referrals
- ○ Suspensions
- ○ Expulsions
- ○ Other data source contextualized to your school: _____

□ **Academic Data**
- ○ State assessment data
- ○ Universal screening data for reading, writing, mathematics
- ○ Enrollment in advanced courses

- o Enrollment in gifted and talented programming
- o Enrollment in special education
- o Participation in extracurricular activities
- o Other data source contextualized to your school: _____

☐ **Early Warning System (EWS) Data**
- o Attendance
- o Behavior (i.e., ODR, suspension)
- o Course Performance

☐ **Behavioral & Mental Health Data**
- o Universal behavioral screening data
- o Tier 2 and 3 intervention enrollment and progress monitoring data
- o Out-of-school placement data for behavioral and/or mental health reasons
- o Referrals to community mental health providers
- o Crisis response and intervention referrals
- o Other data source contextualized to your school: _____

☐ **Perception Data**
- o Student perception of school climate data
- o Family and community perception of school climate data
- o School personnel perception of school climate data
- o Other data source contextualized to your school: _____

Community Resources Audit

What is the name, location, and contact information for the organization?	What services are provided?	What populations are served?	How are services initiated?	Does our school have a partnership with this organization?

3

Implementation and Evaluation

A Conceptual Framework of Sustained Implementation

Most educators who have spent a few years working in public schools experience the ebb and flow of educational initiatives, with many suggesting that if one waits long enough, the latest initiative will likely wane into nonexistence in a few years. While this may not necessarily be a bad thing, particularly if the new initiative is not evidence-based, such life-and-death cycles of initiatives that actually produce positive outcomes for students, teachers, and communities are tragic.

Latham (1988) operationalized this cycle of educational initiatives to last about 5 years. Initially enthusiasm is high and provides fertile ground for adoption of an educational initiative. That enthusiasm, however, diminishes in less than 5 years and often is coincidentally associated with a change in building-level leadership. Thus, most educational initiatives fizzle out in less than 5 years. This 5-year life cycle is especially problematic for school-wide initiatives given the fruits of those labors do not typically materialize until at least 3 years of sustained, high-fidelity implementation (Castillo & Curtis, 2014; Fixsen et al., 2005). Therefore, it is important to understand the process of initially adopting and sustaining a school-wide effort such as positive

DOI: 10.4324/9781003294351-3

behavioral interventions and supports (PBIS) to ensure that all that effort bears fruit for students, staff, and communities.

The National Implementation Research Network (NIRN, 2013, 2020) produced one of the most influential summaries regarding the implementation of evidence-based practices across a variety of disciplines (e.g., education, juvenile justice, mental health, social services). Aggregation of the literature across fields coalesced into a conceptual framework that is widely accepted in the social sciences, including education, and informs assessment and action planning around adoption and sustained implementation of any large-scale effort. To that end, this work is informative to PBIS.

Fixsen and colleagues (2005) argued that "implementation is a process, not an event" (p. 15) and is often manifested in evidence-based practices being installed in fits and spurts. In other words, the process of installing an evidence-based framework such as PBIS will occur in a curvilinear manner, not a smooth or gradual one (Chamberlain et al., 2011; Panzano & Roth, 2006). Anecdotally, such can be the case with PBIS as teams are initially trained and have intense motivation and enthusiasm to install tier 1 PBIS. In some instances, however, this does not necessarily translate to high-fidelity implementation even 1–2 years after tier 1 professional development training is delivered.

The reality that implementation of any evidence-based practice is nonlinear underscores the importance of NIRN's (2020) conceptual framework of the stages of the implementation process. Having an understanding of the stages of implementation is not only insightful for the initial adoption of an evidence-based practice such as PBIS, but it is informative for sustaining and expanding the practice to other settings across an organization. Thus, a review of this conceptual framework is provided along with its application to PBIS.

The first stage of implementation, termed *Exploration*, occurs when individuals within an organization recognize the need to do something different, to consider some innovative practice with the hopes of achieving a desired, albeit currently elusive, outcome. Once the motivation to do something different materializes, an appraisal is made to determine the extent to which there is a match between the needs of the organization, resources, and availability of evidence-based practices. The conclusion of this Exploration stage is the determination of whether to implement an innovative evidence-based practice (NIRN, 2020).

The second stage of implementation is called *Installation*. Resources are allocated to install the agreed upon evidence-based practice during this stage. Resources include financial and human capital, professional development, technology, space, and policy/procedural changes that all support the eventual installation of the evidence-based practice. The result of this stage of implementation is the organization's capacity to begin initial adoption of the evidence-based practice (NIRN, 2020).

The third stage of implementation, the *Initial Implementation* stage, is marked by early adoption of the evidence-based practice; however, common challenges to implementation fidelity including competing priorities, diminished enthusiasm, staff turnover, and other forces are prominent. Consequently, initial implementation can be rather tenuous for those first few years (Fixsen et al., 2005; NIRN, 2013, 2020). But if the organization manages to stay the course by focusing on implementation and mitigating barriers to implementation, progression into the fourth stage is highly likely.

At the fourth stage of implementation, *Full Implementation*, the innovative evidence-based practice is now firmly rooted as standard operating procedure. It is no longer a novel or innovative practice but one that is fully integrated into the organization's daily functioning. When this occurs, the evidence-based practice is fully embraced by staff and the policies and procedures that support implementation are well established. Notably, it is at this point that the anticipated positive outcomes that initially motivated the organization toward change during the Exploration phase come to fruition (Castillo & Curtis, 2014; NIRN, 2020).

After fully implementing an evidence-based practice, innovation of the routinized, formerly novel, evidence-based practice is needed to suit the unique needs and characteristics of the organization. Elements of the practice that are deemed ineffective are abandoned and innovations to the practice are common while still keeping true to the core features of the original, evidence-based practice (Fixsen et al., 2005). In doing so, the evolution of the evidence-based practice is a product of the idiosyncratic features of the organization often resulting in even more positive outcomes.

The ultimate goal of achieving full implementation of an evidence-based practice that has been innovated to meet the unique needs of the organization is long-term sustainability. This is exemplified by multi-year implementation of the evidence-based practice even in the face of staff turnover, changes in administrative leadership, and disruptions to original implementation resources (e.g., funding, professional development, expert support). Despite all these internal and external forces that would otherwise sabotage sustained implementation, organizations that reach this stage tend to weather just about any storm. Fundamentally, organizations at this stage have achieved "long-term survival and continued . . . implementation . . . in the context of a changing world" (Fixsen et al., 2005, p. 17).

Adoption and Sustained Implementation of PBIS

We now apply NIRN's (2020) conceptual framework to PBIS as a means to help expand sustained implementation of this evidence-based framework across organizations such as preschools and PreK–12 schools. While early work related to adopting PBIS in PreK–12 schools was informative (e.g., Bambara et al., 2009; Coffey & Horner, 2012), the work by Kent McIntosh and colleagues over the past decade provides not only the theoretical understanding of sustained School-Wide PBIS (SWPBIS) implementation but also the tools to measure and inform data-based action planning to increase the probability of sustaining and expanding SWPBIS. Appraisal of the degree to which schools have installed SWPBIS and the various factors that enable or prevent adoption and sustain implementation of tier 1 SWPBIS is accomplished via the *School-Wide Universal Behavior Sustainability Index: School Teams* (SUBSIST; McIntosh et al., 2009). More recently, a companion tool, called the *Advanced Level Tier Interventions Treatment Utilization and Durability Evaluation* (ALTITUDE; Kittelman et al., 2021), was created to assess enablers and barriers to sustained implementation of advanced tiers (i.e., tier 2 and tier 3). Both the SUBSIST and ALTITUDE have undergone rigorous investigation to establish their psychometric qualities, resulting in the designation of both as high-quality and helpful tools in understanding how to sustain SWP-BIS across the tiers.

Adopting Tier 1 SWPBIS

Bradshaw and Pas (2011) found that one of the primary motivations for schools to enter into the SWPBIS Exploration stage is out of a concern for the welfare of students, staff, and community. Among the chief reasons for schools to even consider SWPBIS is high rates of exclusionary discipline practices (e.g., office discipline referrals, out-of-school suspensions) and poor academic performance. Not surprisingly, many schools in our experience explore and initially adopt SWPBIS because of similar challenges experienced in their schools.

But specific to this focal point of this book is our encouragement that schools explore SWPBIS as an approach to address equity for all students. While that early work (e.g., Bradshaw & Pas, 2011) did not necessarily consider disproportionate discipline as another motivator for exploring and adopting SWPBIS, it is reasonable to hypothesize this given three decades of work illustrating the severity and chronicity of such practices toward minoritized groups (Gage et al., 2021; Skiba et al., 1997; Townsend, 2000). Additionally, the recent emphasis on equity and social justice in a broader sense (e.g., academic opportunities, graduation rates, poverty) should undoubtedly motivate schools to consider SWPBIS as a framework to make schools work for all students by increasing the probability that minoritized groups experience high rates of educational success. Therefore, we anticipate many schools would consider SWPBIS as part of the comprehensive solution to providing equitable outcomes for all students, whether those be academic, social, emotional, or behavioral outcomes.

Once a commitment to installing SWPBIS is made, however, resources must be allocated and activities must occur to initially install the framework (i.e., Installation stage). McIntosh et al., (2013) highlighted the adequacy of funding, provision of high-quality professional development, and availability of expertise and effective coaching as critical to the initial adoption of tier 1 SWPBIS. One can imagine that these important enablers of initial adoption must be present at both the building level and at the central office level given resources and professional development are often under the purview of district administration. Therefore, key to initial adoption of tier 1 SWPBIS is building-level and district-level administrative support. It is expected that administrators, educators, the local community, and aligned community-based partners commit to supporting what is needed to achieve initial adoption. The Pennsylvania Positive Behavior Support Network (PAPBS Network) offers an example of such commitments made by the school district and agency partners (https://papbs.org/Portals/0/UploadedFiles/2_PAPBS_Commitment_to_Fidelity_Imple mentation%2006%2015%2015.pdf). Illustrated in this document is, among many things, a commitment to a multi-year training/professional development series, on-site coaching and technical assistance provided by experts, allocation of financial resources, full staff buy-in, and agreement to collect and analyze fidelity and outcome data. Not only are these commitments practically relevant, per the NIRN (2020) stages of implementation framework, but they are also empirically derived from the recent work of McIntosh and colleagues specific to SWPBIS.

Initial implementation of tier 1 SWPBIS occurs once resources are activated, professional development has occurred, and the infrastructure, including policies and procedures, are built and installed (i.e., Initial Implementation stage). Initially staff are enthusiastic about SWPBIS adoption and are highly motivated to install the practices. But initial SWPBIS installation, however, does not equate to sustained implementation (Latham, 1988). SWPBIS is not immune to the same barriers to initial adoption as other evidence-based practices, including distractions toward other initiatives, waning enthusiasm, or the loss of keystone administrators and/or staff. This appears to be particularly acute in secondary schools. It seems that the unique features of high schools compared to elementary schools, such as high schools often being much larger, faculty and staff at high schools creating organizational cultures and climates that differ from elementary schools, and high school students' developmental level makes high school implementation more challenging with longer latency from initial training to implementation fidelity (Flannery & McGrath Kato, 2017; McIntosh et al., 2018). Thus, it appears that SWPBIS likely follows the same non-linear implementation trajectory as other evidence-based practices and might be especially so in secondary schools.

Thankfully, a growing body of evidence specific to SWPBIS has emerged that is informative to achieving initial adoption. McIntosh et al., (2013) reported that making SWPBIS a district and building priority increases the probability of initial implementation. Designation of sufficient resources to train and install SWPBIS are also positive indicators of high-fidelity implementation. In a separate study, McIntosh et al., (2014) noted that administrative support, a functioning SWPBIS school team, and parent support are also essential to early adoption of the framework. Additionally, as will be described in more depth when reviewing the critical features of reaching the Full Implementation stage, a number of practices in the early years of implementation should be of particular emphasis. These include regularly scheduled SWPBIS team meetings and the omnipresence of data and data analyses to drive implementation efforts (Hume & McIntosh, 2013; McIntosh et al., 2018). It thus appears that these characteristics and practices are essential to achieving the Initial Implementation stage of SWPBIS as well as predictive of longer-term implementation. Consequently, this evidentiary support provides compelling justification for securing commitments from all stakeholder groups early on in the Exploration phase, such as what occurs with the PAPBS Network, to achieve Initial Implementation of SWPBIS.

Sustaining Tier 1 SWPBIS

Achieving initial implementation of SWPBIS is something to be celebrated; however, the implementation work is not finished. Runge and colleagues (Runge et al., 2020), using data from the PAPBS Network, observed that a minority of schools initially adopt SWPBIS for a year or two but then succumb to what is likely many of the same barriers to sustained implementation conceptualized by Latham (1988) and empirically established by McIntosh and colleagues (Hume & McIntosh, 2013; McIntosh et al., 2013, 2018). Therefore, achieving NIRN's (2020) Full Implementation stage requires additional work. The fantastic news, however, is that we have evidence to help schools achieve this stage of implementation, where SWPBIS is no longer a set of novel practices but simply how the school regularly operates.

Achievement of Full Implementation means SWPBIS is assimilated into the daily operating procedure of the school. Again, McIntosh's and colleagues' (2014, 2018) work is incredibly insightful in that the evidentiary support all points to, paradoxically, a small number of critical characteristics and practices that predict achieving Full Implementation status. One of the strongest predictors of implementation of SWPBIS for three or more years is, not surprisingly, the extent to which the framework was initially installed with fidelity (McIntosh et al., 2018). In other words, schools that start out implementing SWPBIS very well will likely do so much more than schools that meander haphazardly toward eventual implementation fidelity. Administrative support is also critical to initial adoption and achieving Full Implementation stage (McIntosh et al., 2014). But equally strong predictors of multi-year tier 1 SWPBIS implementation are the extent to which the SWPBIS team meets regularly, discusses data, and makes decisions about implementation efforts based on those data. Hence, as noted earlier, schools initially installing SWPBIS would be wise to place particular emphasis on the SWPBIS team meeting regularly, systematic data collection and analysis, and use of those analyses to action plan around implementation efforts from the very beginning so that these practices are firmly established (McIntosh et al., 2014, 2018). Such practices, as noted earlier, will support Initial Implementation as well as Full Implementation across multiple years.

These essential features of Initial Implementation and Full Implementation will bode well for the equity work central to this book given the emphasis on objective data and unabashedly honest discussions around data to inform the practices necessary to achieve equity for all students. As will be reviewed later in this chapter, there are specific data metrics that can be analyzed to inform the extent to which SWPBIS practices are achieving their intended outcomes for all students. Favorable data are used to justify existing practices and sustain them moving forward. Unfavorable data are used to modify, if not abandon, existing practices. Therefore, placing an emphasis on these practices key to initial adoption and sustained implementation will concurrently assist with the important equity work that needs to be done.

Given that students spend the majority of the school day in classrooms receiving instruction, it is not surprising to note that the quality of PBIS practices implemented in the classroom setting is another predictor of sustained implementation (Mathews et al., 2014). More specifically, the explicit teaching of behaviors and expectations, the extent to which there is a match between teacher instruction and students' skills, and teachers' access to behavioral supports are highly predictive of both initial and sustained SWPBIS implementation (i.e., Initial Implementation; Full Implementation). These findings, while perhaps obvious to some, underscore the importance of implementing SWPBIS practices in the context in which most student misbehavior occurs and when academic learning should be optimized: the classroom. In fact, Han and Weiss (2005) theorized that the actions of individual teachers are most important for sustainability of *any* effort. Thus it appears this is also true of SWPBIS. The more teachers engage in PBIS practices in their classrooms, the more likely that SWPBIS will be sustained for multiple years. Consequently, maintaining Full Implementation of SWPBIS requires a particular focus on ensuring classroom practices are consistent with the school-wide framework.

Interestingly, McIntosh's and colleagues' (2015, 2018) work reveals that school characteristics one might think would be barriers to sustained implementation of SWPBIS (i.e., Full Implementation) are not empirically supported. Namely, the level of community poverty (i.e., free or reduced meal status of students) and school size do not predict SWPBIS sustainability. Additionally, the demographic constitution of the student body is not associated with an increased risk for failing to sustain SWPBIS implementation. This is highly encouraging given that some of our most needy schools and schools that struggle to achieve equitable outcomes for all students are those that are considered high-poverty schools and/or are in majority minority communities. Additionally, many, but certainly not all, of our neediest schools are those with large student enrollments. Given work by McIntosh and colleagues, such school/community characteristics are not harbingers of failed SWPBIS implementation. There is, however, one school characteristic relevant to predicting sustained tier 1 SWPBIS implementation: building level. McIntosh's and colleagues' work indicates that sustained implementation over multiple years is much more difficult at the secondary level. While it is possible for a secondary school to achieve Full Implementation status, these contexts apparently have substantively more implementation barriers than elementary schools. Despite these challenges, data suggest that if a secondary school can implement SWPBIS for 3 years, it is highly likely that they, similar to their elementary counterparts, can achieve the Innovation stage of implementation.

Sustaining Full Implementation status will undoubtedly be supported through innovation over subsequent years (Fixen et al., 2005). Schools that achieve SWPBIS implementation for multiple years begin to adapt practices to better align with the unique characteristics and needs of the local community. Ideally, these innovations are installed because the data collected thus far suggest that a particular feature of tier 1 SWPBIS should be added, modified, or abandoned. One such common occurrence in our experience is the adoption of a social-emotional learning (SEL) curriculum to explicitly teach students those critical skills that are not the primary focus on traditional tier 1 SWPBIS. These skills include self-awareness, self-management, social awareness, relationship skills, and responsible decision-making (Collaborative for Academic, Social, and Emotional Learning [CASEL], 2022). In fact, some leaders in the field of SEL argue that SWPBIS and SEL are complementary and, when combined, strengthen outcomes for students (Bear, 2010; Bear et al., 2015). In these situations, schools are wise to consider innovating only with SEL curricula that are evidence-based, such as those endorsed by CASEL (n.d.; e.g., Promoting Alternative THinking Strategies; 4Rs; Building Assets, Reducing Risks; I Can Problem Solve; Incredible Years; Second Step; Social Skills Improvement System Classroom Intervention Program).

Another example of innovation is the increased participation and voice of families and students, as appropriate (McIntosh et al., 2014). This is not to suggest that these voices are muted or ignored in the early adoption and implementation stages, but a concerted effort should now occur to expand the inclusion of other stakeholder groups. In our experience, these voices tend to be meaningfully added after a school has fully implemented tier 1 SWPBIS for a few years. Not only does this create a more inclusive SWPBIS framework but often is more culturally relevant to the students and families, particularly when the school staff come from cultural or linguistic backgrounds and experiences that are considerably different from the local community.

Another SWPBIS innovation that we see occurring at this stage, and one that is central to the focus of this text, is taking a critical view of equity as a by-product of the multi-year installation of tier 1 SWPBIS. Given that, by this time, tier 1 SWPBIS has been implemented for at least 3 years, data processes and practices should be well established to evaluate the extent to which desired outcomes are realized (Castillo & Curtis, 2014; Fixsen et al., 2005; NIRN, 2020). This would especially be true given key indicators of Full Implementation status, as noted earlier, include data teams that regularly meet and the reliance on data to action plan implementation efforts (McIntosh et al., 2014, 2018). Specific to equity, therefore, might be a desire to innovate existing teacher and administrative practices around addressing inappropriate behavior to ensure disciplinary practices are not disproportionately targeting students of color or students with special needs. While this work is challenging, we have witnessed school systems innovate their tier 1 SWPBIS framework to systematically reduce disproportionate discipline (Runge et al., 2017).

Adoption of Advanced Tiers of SWPBIS

It is also at this time that we should expect schools to begin the work of exploring, adopting, and implementing advanced tiers of SWPBIS. While the conceptual issues related to progressing through NIRN's (2020) stages of implementation for advanced tiers of SWPBIS would, theoretically, mirror those of the stages of implementing tier 1 SWPBIS, the empirical evidence to support this is only beginning to emerge. Kittelman and colleagues (2021) recently developed and validated an implementation and sustainability measure for advanced tiers of SWPBIS with their preliminary evidence suggesting very similar enablers of adoption and sustained implementation of advanced tiers as observed in tier 1 SWPBIS (e.g., regular team meetings, use of data to action plan). It is anticipated that future research will further inform the conceptual framework to understand how to adopt, install, and sustain tier 2 and tier 3 SWPBIS. Nonetheless, it is often through innovation of a fully implemented SWPBIS framework that we see schools embarking on the important work of layering on the additional systems, practices, and systems to install and sustain advanced tiers of SWPBIS.

As schools innovate SWPBIS and expand to the advanced tiers, they eventually find themselves proudly sustaining the evidence-based practice over multiple years (e.g., 5+ years) and besting the odds stacked against them by weathering waxing and waning enthusiasm, changes in staff, changes in administration, and changes in building and district priorities. Moreover, we often see tier 1 SWPBIS efforts taking root in other schools across the same school district. That first school to implement SWPBIS—having achieved full implementation and innovation to meet its unique needs—often becomes the demonstration site for other schools to emulate. Importantly, as tier 1 SWPBIS germinates across other schools, these later-adopting schools benefit by learning from and avoiding the challenges faced and overcome by the maiden SWPBIS site. We suspect that this translates into a shorter latency to achieving high-fidelity implementation on the later-adopting schools, although we are not aware of any concrete evidence to support this claim. Intuitively, however, it makes sense, and we have witnessed this anecdotally in Pennsylvanian schools. But fundamentally, schools that reach the Full Implementation phase of implementation and have successfully innovated practices are very likely to maintain high-fidelity implementation of SWPBIS over many years because they have successfully navigated the barriers that would otherwise have undermined implementation while concurrently capitalizing on the enablers to sustained implementation.

As we have hopefully demonstrated, NIRN's (2020) work around implementation science has very concrete applications to SWPBIS. It is hoped that schools, wherever they are along the implementation continuum, can utilize these conceptualized implementation stages and the empirical evidence specific to SWPBIS in an effort to ensure that the hard work resulting in fidelity of implementation not only occurs but is durable. To that end, we advocate for a systematic approach, embedded within the implementation stages, to evaluating SWPBIS across a number of domains so that data are the bedrock of decision-making not only in the daily implementation of SWPBIS (e.g., ODRs) but in the decisions made to sustain and expand this framework.

Evaluation of PBIS

Organizations should critically evaluate the extent to which its priorities are implemented with fidelity and whether the intended positive outcomes materialize. This accountability movement began in earnest with the passing of No Child Left Behind and continues today under the Every Student Succeeds Act. Holding schools accountable is not only important for taxpayers who foot the bill for public education, but, more importantly, for the children educated in schools given our society relies on them to be well prepared for making meaningful contributions as adults. The passage of No Child Left Behind thrust this accountability movement on schools with specific regard to academic outcomes, attendance, and graduation rates. Accounting for the fidelity of PBIS implementation and whether positive outcomes result is no different. Both taxpayers and consumers of educational programming (students) should hold schools to account for their ability to implement and sustain PBIS and achieve positive results. Therefore, we contend that evaluation of PBIS should occur from the very beginning stages of implementation (e.g., Exploration and Installation) through every year of sustained implementation.

PBIS Evaluation Planning Process

The National Center on Positive Behavioral Interventions and Support (Center on PBIS, 2020) developed an Evaluation Blueprint with the expressed intent of its use in large-scale PBIS evaluations, namely state-level evaluations or evaluations of large organizations such as school districts. That said, we believe that this Blueprint provides a helpful roadmap, albeit on a much smaller scale, for the evaluation of PBIS implementation in an organization. We argue that the evaluation cycle underlying large-scale PBIS implementation is still relevant on a smaller scale: *Planning Evaluations, Conducting Evaluations, Reporting Evaluation Results*, and *Using Results for Continuous Improvement*. This cyclical process of conducting evaluations for accountability purposes is not unique to hundreds or even dozens of buildings. It is salient for even one building. Therefore, we recommend referencing this Blueprint for individual organization accountability or organization-wide accountability. A brief summary of this Blueprint, therefore, is provided herein. We begin with a description of how to plan an evaluation.

Planning an evaluation adheres to a somewhat linear progression through six distinct stages. First, the purpose of the evaluation must be established. Often the purpose of PBIS evaluations is to assess, in a summative manner, whether installation is occurring and outcomes are achieved. Another purpose of PBIS evaluation is for accountability, determining whether a priority of the district was achieved, for example. The second step of the evaluation planning process is to identify key stakeholders who will lead the evaluation effort. A wide net should be cast to ensure that all stakeholder groups are included. In the third stage of the evaluation planning process, the evaluation team members are identified. Each member of the evaluation team must have a particular area of expertise that strengthens the quality of the team and the ability to meaningfully and substantively contribute to the evaluation work. For example, the typical constitution of a SWPBIS evaluation team includes central office administrators, building administrators, teacher leaders, district support personnel (e.g., school psychologists, school counselors, school social workers), family members, liaisons with community mental health organizations, and other groups that may have a perspective that is unique to that community (e.g., business, civic, or faith leaders). The fourth step of the evaluation planning process is to establish a timeline for completing the evaluation. With PBIS, this timeline is typically an annual cycle to complete an evaluation from beginning to end. Given the timing at which certain data are collected within a PBIS framework (e.g., fidelity measured in spring; outcome data not available until the school year ends), it is common for these initial stages of evaluation planning to occur in the first half of a calendar year with the remaining stages of the evaluation process occurring in the fall and winter months. The fifth stage of the evaluation planning process is to define the core evaluation questions that will drive the evaluation team's efforts toward producing an evaluation that represents the interests of all stakeholder groups. Evaluation questions specific to PBIS will be expanded on in the following paragraphs. In the sixth and final stage of planning the evaluation, evaluation measures are identified. Again, expansion on this stage of the evaluation process is forthcoming in this chapter. Once these steps have been achieved, then the evaluation team is prepared to formally conduct the evaluation given its predetermined evaluation questions and evaluation measures (Center on PBIS, 2020).

An expansion on the core evaluation questions (step 5) and evaluation measures selected (step 6) is now offered as general guidance to organizations with a specific emphasis on PreK–12 schools; however, the specifics can and should reflect the unique interests, needs, and circumstances of the organization and its constituent stakeholders. Consequently, no two PBIS evaluations should look alike. We witness this at a statewide level with most states evaluating some common outcomes (e.g., fidelity, ODRs) while each evaluates its own unique questions and measures (e.g., Pennsylvania monitors out-of-school educational placements for students with disabilities [Runge et al., 2021]; Missouri evaluates attendance at and satisfaction with professional development [Missouri Schoolwide Positive Behavior Support, 2020]).

Domains of PBIS Evaluation

Once again, the Center on PBIS (2020) Blueprint provides guidance that can be adapted or modified to suit the needs of individual organizations despite the document's intended use for large-scale evaluations. Five broad domains should be considered by the evaluation team as a structure to guide the establishment of observable and measurable evaluative questions: (1) Reach, (2) Process, (3) Capacity, (4) Fidelity, and (5) Outcomes. Our experience has been that most evaluation teams desire to jump straight to outcomes. We contend, however, that the other domains are equally as important and should not be overlooked. Concurrent to our review of these five domains is a consideration for what evaluation measures (data; step 6 of the Planning Process) might be beneficial to the cause. Furthermore, our review that follows focuses on evaluation questions for SWPBIS given much of the work to date on large-scale evaluation of PBIS has been in PreK–12 settings.

Reach

Reach is the extent to which SWPBIS is being practiced in a school or district. Typically, evaluation questions in this domain include the number of schools participating in SWPBIS (applicable if the evaluation is district-wide). Note that this evaluation question and associated counts of schools does not reflect the degree of implementation fidelity. That will be appraised in a later evaluative domain. If applicable, counts of schools by building type (e.g., elementary, middle, high, alternative) could be considered. An account of aligned organizations supporting this work could also be assessed under this domain. Finally, most schools would likely want to report on the number of students educated in school(s) participating in SWPBIS. All of these are typical evaluative questions and measures under the domain of Reach (Center on PBIS, 2020).

Process

The second evaluative domain is *Process*, an assessment of what is occurring with the SWPBIS initiative. Schools might elect to report out what leadership activities have occurred to support implementation, such as policy or procedural changes. An account of professional development activities, including how much training and on-site coaching was offered and who received such support, can be included in this evaluative domain as well. Satisfaction with the professional development activities might also be of interest to evaluation teams. Often this evaluation domain is appraised via data collected from administrative meeting minutes (e.g., policy changes), professional development calendars (e.g., trainings), logs of technical assistance provided (e.g., coaching), and surveys and other feedback from recipients of professional development (e.g., satisfaction).

Capacity

The third evaluative domain recommended by the Center on PBIS (2020), identified as *Capacity*, focuses on the extent to which "the organization can implement and sustain PBIS" (p. 12). Inventories of resources available to support training and installation of SWPBIS might be summarized, including direct financial assistance, allocation of employee full-time equivalents to support SWPBIS, and the participation of aligned community organizations. All of these data speak to the extent to which the school or district has adequate resources to install and sustain SWPBIS.

Fidelity

The fourth evaluative domain recommended by the Center on PBIS (2020) addresses the fidelity with which the tiers of SWPBIS are implemented. This domain, labeled *Fidelity*, is commonly characterized by a summary of how well each tier of SWPBIS was implemented. Summative appraisals of overall tier implementation are accomplished via the following research-validated instruments: *Team Implementation Checklist* (TIC; Sugai et al., 2009), the *Benchmarks of Quality* (BoQ; Kincaid et al., 2010), the *Schoolwide Evaluation Tool* (SET; Sugai et al., 2005), and the *Tiered Fidelity Inventory* (TFI; Algozzine et al., 2014). Additionally, some of these instruments provide factor scores which provide rich information about specific elements of tiered support that are implemented to criterion and specific elements that should be targeted for improvement.

Outcomes

The fifth and often most attention-grabbing SWPBIS evaluative domain is termed *Outcomes* (Center on PBIS, 2020). Broadly, this domain assesses the extent to which SWPBIS implementation is achieving its intended goals. Common student-level outcomes include disciplinary practices (e.g., ODRs, suspensions), academic performance (e.g., state accountability test results), social/emotional screening data (e.g., *Student Risk Screening Scale*; *Pennsylvania Youth Survey*), or attendance or graduation rates. Non-student-level data such as indicators of school climate, referrals to special education, staff perceptions of safety or behavioral support across all environments, or perceptions of families and community members might also be assessed in this domain.

Importance of Fidelity

Note that across all measures appraised in the Outcome domain, fidelity of implementation must provide the backdrop or context through which all data must be interpreted. In fact, it is our contention that the only time outcome data relative to a year in which SWPBIS was not implemented with fidelity should be analyzed and reported is when the evaluation team specifically identifies those data as corresponding to baseline (i.e., pre-implementation). Categorizing outcomes specifically as occurring during baseline will facilitate important pre-post comparisons of a specific outcome to determine the extent to which SWPBIS can be associated with the observed changes in that outcome. At no other time, however, should baseline data be reported. Subsequent to installation of SWPBIS, then, the evaluation report should clearly identify which outcome data correspond to years during which SWPBIS was installed with fidelity.

Equity

Specific to the central focus of this book is the need to analyze and report outcome data through an equity lens. When possible, outcome data disaggregated by marginalized or minoritized groups will offer objective appraisals of the extent to which all groups are achieving similar goals and, in the case of action planning for improvement, provide a means by which to monitor when gaps in outcomes are closing. Considerations might include groups based on race, special education status, or identification as LGBTQ. To view outcomes through an equity lens, evaluative teams need to familiarize themselves with and create systems that support the collection of data disaggregated by groups (e.g., race, special education status). Typically, such systems already exist, especially with regard to ODRs and suspensions (e.g., *School-Wide Information System*). But similar data systems might need to be developed to support this work around other outcomes such as academic performance, social/emotional health, or attendance or graduation rates.

Two key metrics are salient to the work around appraising equity of outcomes. Originally applied in the medical community (Vogt, 2005), use of risk indices expanded to reveal disproportionate membership in special education and restrictive educational placements for students of color (e.g., Skiba et al., 2006, 2008). More recently, these metrics are recommended for examining the proportionality of disciplinary actions taken against students who exhibit disruptive behavior (Boneshefski & Runge, 2014). Because of their roots in medicine, the metrics are identified as indicators of risk although they can be used for identifying the extent to which a group achieves/receives a positive outcome, such as access to AP courses or graduation rates (Bollmer et al., 2007; Mcloughlin & Noltemeyer, 2010). Regardless of whether the outcome is negative or positive, the formulae and interpretations are the same.

The first equity metric is known as the *Risk Index*. A risk index represents the proportion of a group that experiences a particular outcome (e.g., ODR, suspension). Calculation of a risk index is straightforward: the number of students in a particular group who receive an outcome (e.g., suspension) divided by the total number of students in that particular group (see Figure 3.1). Risk indices should be calculated for all groups, as these data are necessary for computing the subsequent equity metric (risk ratios); however, due to privacy, risk indices of groups with less than ten students should not be reported (Boneshefski & Runge, 2014; Data Accountability Center, 2011).

Determining the extent to which a risk index is too high, too low, or appropriate, however, is unclear given the disproportionate influence small group sizes have on the computed risk index relative to risk indices calculated with much larger groups of students. Therefore, a second equity metric must be calculated to facilitate appropriate cross-group comparisons of risk. This metric is called a *Risk Ratio* and is calculated by dividing the risk index of a particular group with the risk index of all other groups (see Figure 3.2). The resulting metric is interpreted as an indicator of relative risk of one group compared to all other groups.

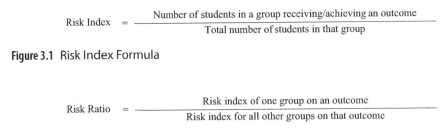

$$\text{Risk Index} \; = \; \frac{\text{Number of students in a group receiving/achieving an outcome}}{\text{Total number of students in that group}}$$

Figure 3.1 Risk Index Formula

$$\text{Risk Ratio} \; = \; \frac{\text{Risk index of one group on an outcome}}{\text{Risk index for all other groups on that outcome}}$$

Figure 3.2 Risk Ratio Formula

The basic interpretation of risk ratios is simple. A risk ratio of 1.0 indicates the particular group receives/achieves the outcome at the same rate as all other groups of students. Risk ratios below 1.0 indicate lower rates than all other student groups, while risk ratios above 1.0 indicate higher rates than all other student groups. The further away from 1.0, the greater the magnitude of risk relative to all other student groups. Unfortunately, there is no consensus on what constitutes an unacceptably high or low risk ratio. This is likely due, in part, to the relative importance or significance of outcomes for which risk ratios are computed. For example, a risk ratio of 1.50 may be viewed as relatively benign for an outcome like self-referrals to the nurse's office, but that same risk ratio for suspension rates may be very concerning and in need of action planning. Consequently, it is important for evaluation teams to establish *a priori* what constitutes a risk ratio that is unacceptable.

Conclusion

We argue that implementation of the tiers of SWPBIS is challenging but can occur at all grade levels. We also acknowledge that NIRN's (2020) conceptualization of the stages of implementation are applicable to SWPBIS with schools initially becoming interested in doing something different to affect positive change for students and the school community. Through systematic allocation and utilization of resources, schools can initially implement tier 1 SWPBIS. Key features of tier 1 SWPBIS, namely administrative support, regular team meetings, and use of data to make decisions about implementation, will not only predict the quality of initial implementation but also the probability of long-term sustained implementation. After a few years of implementing tier 1 SWPBIS, schools make appropriate adaptations to their framework to meet the unique needs and characteristics of the school while simultaneously embarking on the critical work of layering on advanced tiers of SWPBIS. Eventually, schools that sustain multiple years of high-fidelity SWPBIS implementation no longer view the framework as a novel approach; rather, it is part of standard operating procedure for the school.

Concurrent to the stages of implementation is the importance we place on ensuring a systematic annual evaluation led by a group of stakeholders who manage a pre-established set of milestones that must be achieved over the course of a calendar year. Two of those milestones, establishing evaluation questions and measurements, require careful consideration of what matters most to stakeholders and the feasibility of obtaining data to answer those evaluative questions.

Conducting an annual evaluation of SWPBIS should focus on Reach, Process, Capacity, Fidelity, and Outcomes as this comprehensive approach will assess current practices and support the life of the framework beyond the 5-year life-death cycle of initiatives typical in educational reform (Latham, 1988). Reach, Process, and Capacity are just as important to the evaluation plan as Fidelity and Outcomes although the latter two often receive the most attention. Furthermore, it is important that all outcomes are evaluated through the context of the degree to which the tiers of SWPBIS were implemented with fidelity. Outcome data absent an articulation of implementation fidelity render interpretations as meaningless at best, erroneous at worst. Finally, use of risk indices and ratios will be essential to understanding the extent to which equitable outcomes occur for all students, including students of color. Moreover, these metrics can be useful in the evaluation of the extent to which efforts at achieving equity are realized.

Chapter 3: Seeds for Growth

- ◆ A **conceptual framework for implementing an evidence-based practice** such as SWPBIS is assistive as teams navigate the stages of implementation.
- ◆ This framework is helpful in **identifying enablers and barriers** to implementation.
- ◆ Regular **appraisal of implementation fidelity** helps to identify these enablers and barriers to implementation.
- ◆ **Annual evaluations** of SWPBIS efforts are important to the adoption and sustained implementation of SWPBIS.

◆ An **evaluation team** comprised of members representing **multiple stakeholder groups** should be convened to conduct annual evaluations of SWPBIS.

◆ A comprehensive evaluation framework in which **five domains** and **subsequent evaluation questions** are considered by the evaluation team will be important for the viability of SWPBIS over many years.

◆ Use of available, extant data regarding **reach, process, capacity, fidelity,** and **outcomes** should be capitalized upon within this evaluation process.

◆ A focus on **metrics to assess equitable outcomes** will assist teams in making sound decisions based on objective data.

Vignette/Example

The Anywhere School District is categorized as an urban/suburban public school district 7 miles from a large, metropolitan downtown area. The Anywhere School District has 11 elementary schools, two middle schools, and one high school. The district educates over 12,500 students and has a diverse student population with regard to race: 47% Black/African American, 22% White, 16% Asian, 11% Hispanic/Latinx, 4% Multi-Racial, and <1% American Indian/Alaskan Native. Nearly 100% of the student population receives free or reduced meals. State accountability results reflect a district that, on average, has less than 50% of its students achieving proficient/advanced on end-of-year English Language Arts, Mathematics, and Science tests. The following are excerpted sections of an annual evaluation of SWPBIS implementation across the district with a focus on the district's demonstration site, L. Whitmer Elementary School.

Reach

Administrators and staff at Anywhere School District recognized the need to change how they supported the social, emotional, and behavioral needs of all their students throughout the 2015–2016 academic year following some self-reflection on disparate opportunities, access, and academic outcomes for minoritized students. Initial exploration of SWPBIS occurred at one elementary school in 2015–2016 (L. Whitmer Elementary School) with staff training commencing in 2016–2017. Installation of tier 1 SWPBIS occurred at that school in 2017–2018, as evidenced by fidelity data reported later in this chapter. Since that time, the remaining elementary schools were trained in either 2018–2019 (Lincoln, Eisenhower, South Davis, Jamestown, Willow Hill Elementary Schools) or 2019–2020 (Gage, Ninth Street, Windom, Jackson, and Horace Mann Elementary Schools). Training at the two middle schools is scheduled to occur in 2021–2022 with the high school receiving tier 1 training in 2022–2023. The district has partnered with three mental health agencies to provide consultative services at tier 1 and consultation and direct service at the advanced tiers of SWPBIS.

L. Whitmer Elementary School serves as the district's demonstration site. The school educates over 500 students with almost 100% of the student population receiving free or reduced meals. School and student characteristics are summarized in Table 3.1.

Table 3.1 Demographic characteristics of L. Whitmer Elementary School

Characteristic	Proportion of Student Population
Black/African American	73%
Hispanic/Latinx	10%
White	9%
Multi-Racial	7%
Asian	2%
Free or reduced meals	99%
Special education	19%
Proficient/Advanced English Language Arts	17%
Proficient/Advanced Mathematics	6%
Proficient/Advanced Science	38%

Note. Percentages may not sum to 100% due to rounding

Process

Anywhere School District central and building-level administrators elected to track certain resources needed to train and install SWPBIS in the demonstration school so that these data could be used to project and budget resource allocations as SWPBIS was replicated in other schools over time. The number of training and technical assistance events and amount of time dedicated to these activities over a 4-year period at L. Whitmer Elementary School is provided in Figure 3.3. As evidenced in those data, the year prior to implementation (2016–2017) not surprisingly required the greatest number of training and technical assistance events as well as cumulative hours of support. Since that first year, the number of events and cumulative hours declined. Notably, training and technical assistance dedicated to advanced tiers commenced in 2018–2019, with the majority of resources from that year forward dedicated almost entirely to tier 2 and tier 3 SWPBIS. After 5 years, the number of training and technical assistance events reduced by 60%. Moreover, the amount of time needed to complete training and technical assistance was reduced by 56%.

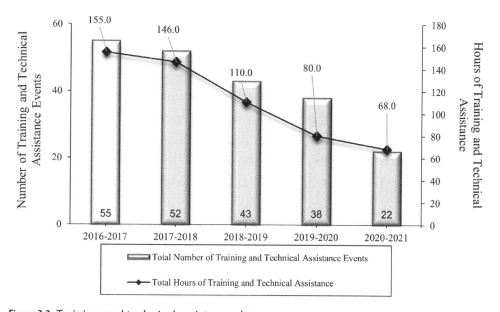

Figure 3.3 Training and technical assistance data

Capacity

Direct financial assistance to support training and technical assistance to L. Whitmer Elementary School staff included a $3,000 start-up grant from the Some State Department of Education in 2016–2017. Subsequent to that year, the principal of L. Whitmer Elementary School allocated, on average, $1,500 toward SWPBIS resources, most of which were used for the reinforcement system (i.e., token economy back-up reinforcers). The Anywhere School District hired a full-time PBIS coordinator for the district in 2016–2017 at an annual cost of approximately $110,000, including benefits. Additional resources to train and provide technical assistance to staff at L. Whitmer Elementary School were included in the annual professional development calendar and budget for the district; therefore, no additional costs or staff to install SWPBIS were needed above and beyond that which was already noted. All of these data speak to the extent to which the school or district has adequate resources to install and sustain SWPBIS.

Fidelity

Implementation of SWPBIS was assessed during the Installation stage (i.e., 2016–2017 academic year) via quarterly completed TICs. Staff used the TIC because of its utility in monitoring the development of infrastructure and practices to eventually install SWPBIS. With initial implementation occurring in 2017–2018, the team switched to the BoQ and TFI as its annual assessments of tier 1 fidelity given this measure assesses tier 1 and advanced tiers of SWPBIS. The BoQ was used because it offers data about specific practices known to support and sustain tier 1 SWPBIS. Furthermore, the TFI was also used to facilitate longitudinal appraisal of advanced tier implementation even though the school had not yet developed the infrastructure and practices of advanced tiers of SWPBIS during the 2017–2018 academic year.

Figure 3.4 reflects tier 1 SWPBIS fidelity data across years and from different fidelity measures, from the Installation stage (2016–2017), to the Initial Implementation stage (2017–2018), and throughout multiple years of tier 1 Full Implementation (2018–2019 through 2020–2021). As is reflected in these data, development and installation of the policies, procedures, practices, and data systems necessary to implement tier 1 SWPBIS occurred during the 2016–2017 academic year (2016–2017;

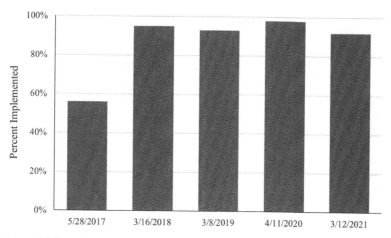

Figure 3.4 Tier 1 fidelity data

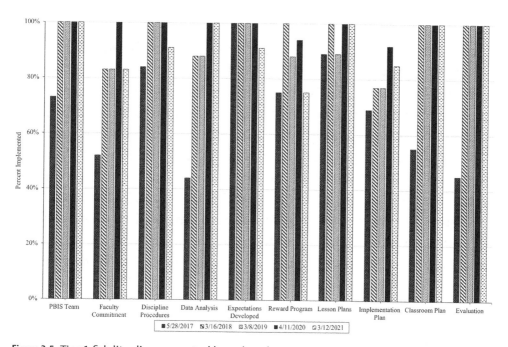

Figure 3.5 Tier 1 fidelity disaggregated by subscale

Installation stage), which, for analyses of outcomes provided in a later section of this summary, is considered a baseline year. Tier 1 SWPBIS was achieved in 2017–2018 and sustained for four consecutive years.

Data in Figure 3.5 provide a longitudinal view of BoQ data disaggregated by factors as a mechanism for the tier 1 team to monitor and sustain enabling factors over multiple years and ensure that those

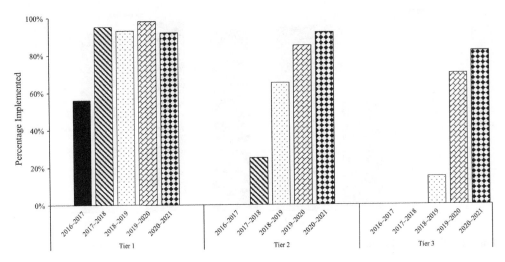

Figure 3.6 Longitudinal data of fidelity across all tiers

procedures and practices that initially were not fully installed, such as Faculty Commitment and Data Analysis, could be bolstered in subsequent years. Not surprisingly, most of the BoQ factors were rated low to moderate during the Installation stage (aka baseline; 2016–2017) with most factors well established in the subsequent year or two. The downward trend of the data regarding the Reward Program suggested to the team that it is necessary to revisit the token economy system for the upcoming year so that this trend can be reversed.

Figure 3.6 depicts the fidelity of implementation of all tiers of SWPBIS across the years. Note that the data in this figure regarding tier 1 are the same as in Figure 3.4. The added benefit of this figure, however, is the assessment of advanced tiers of SWPBIS. Training to develop the infrastructure and practices for advanced tiers occurred in earnest during the 2017–2018 academic year, although as is indicated in the figure, implementation of advanced tiers was relatively low at that time. Beginning in 2018–2019, fidelity of tier 2 SWPBIS was achieved with the criterion achieved for tier 3 SWPBIS in the subsequent year.

Outcomes

Figure 3.7 provides an illustration of a school's multi-year monitoring of ODR data across baseline and multiple years of tier 1 SWPBIS

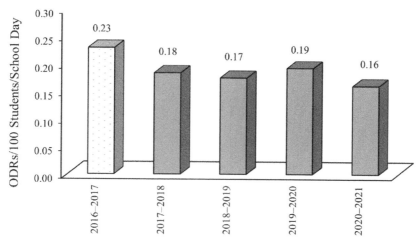

Figure 3.7 Longitudinal office discipline referral data
Note. ODR = office discipline referral. Data from 2016–2017 represent baseline rates with all other years representing data when the school was implementing tier 1 SWPBIS.

implementation. As evidenced by the longitudinal trend, this school witnessed a multi-year downward trend of ODRs. A visual display such as this provides easy-to-understand and empirically validating support for the continuation of SWPBIS.

An alternate display of longitudinal data that concurrently plots fidelity data to demonstrate the relationship between changes in an outcome over time and the degree of implementation is provided in Figure 3.8. Unlike the Figure 3.7, Figure 3.8 has the added feature providing the proportion to fidelity criterion measured each spring. This facilitates an analysis not only of longitudinal changes in out-of-school suspensions but how trends were inversely related to fidelity. In other words, the better tier 1 SWPBIS was implemented, per the annual fidelity measure, the lower the out-of-school suspension (OSS) rate.

An example of a longitudinal analysis of risk ratios for a school is provided in Figure 3.9. A school that initially was not implementing tier 1 SWPBIS established baseline risk ratios for ODRs. Those data clearly indicated disproportionate ODRs for students of color. Consequently, the school embarked on a long-term, systematic plan to address these disparities and continued to monitor their discipline data over the next few years. While the risk ratios did not reach

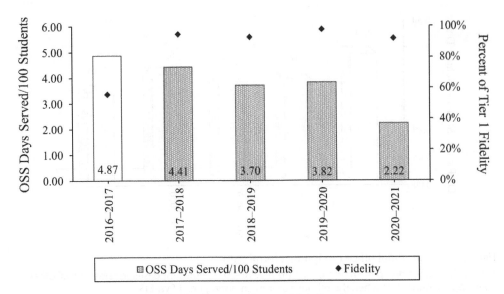

Figure 3.8 Longitudinal out-of-school suspension and fidelity data

Note. OSS = out-of-school suspension. Data from 2016–2017 represent baseline rates with all other years representing data when the school was implementing tier 1 SWPBIS.

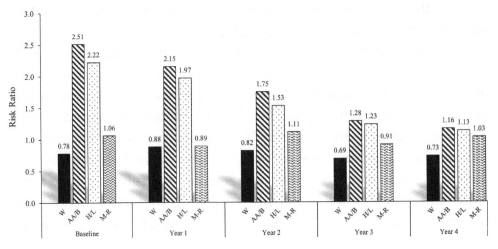

Figure 3.9 Longitudinal equity data report

Note. W = White; AA/B = African American/Black; H/L = Hispanic/Latinx; M-R = Multi-Racial.

1.0 for all groups in that period of time, clearly improvements were observed. These data then provided the support needed to continue implementing the training and coaching that initially resulted in the 3-year decline in risk ratios.

Reference List

Algozzine, B., Barrett, S., Eber, L., George, H., Horner, R., Lewis, T., Putnam, B., Swain-Bradway, J., McIntosh, K., & Sugai, G. (2014). *School-wide PBIS tiered fidelity inventory*. National Technical Assistance Center on Positive Behavioral Interventions and Supports. www.pbis.org

Bambara, L., Nonnemacher, S., & Kern, L. (2009). Sustaining school-based individualized positive behavior support: Perceived barriers and enablers. *Journal of Positive Behavior Interventions, 11*(3), 161–178. https://doi.org/10.1177/1098300708330878

Bear, G. G. (2010). *School discipline and self-discipline: A practical guide to promoting prosocial student behavior*. Guilford.

Bear, G. G., Whitcomb, S. A., Elias, M. J., & Blank, J. (2015). SEL and schoolwide positive behavioral interventions and supports. In J. A. Durlak, C. E. Domitrovich, R. P. Weissberg, & T. P. Gullota (Eds.), *Handbook of social and emotional learning: Research and practice* (pp. 453–467). Guilford.

Bollmer, J., Bethel, J., Garrison-Mogren, R., & Brauen, M. (2007). Using the risk ratio to assess racial/ethnic disproportionality in special education at the school-district level. *The Journal of Special Education, 41*(3), 186–198. https://doi.org/10.1177/00224669070410030401

Boneshefski, M. J., & Runge, T. J. (2014). Addressing disproportionate discipline practices within a school-wide positive behavioral interventions and supports framework: A practical guide for calculating disproportionality rates. *Journal of Positive Behavior Interventions, 16*(3), 149–158. https://doi.org/10.1177/1098300713484064

Bradshaw, C. P., & Pas, E. T. (2011). A state-wide scale-up of positive behavioral interventions and supports (PBIS): A description of the development of systems of support and analysis of adoption and implementation. *School Psychology Review, 40*(4), 530–548. https://doi.org/10.1080/02796015.2011.12087528

Castillo, J. M., & Curtis, M. J. (2014). Best practices in systems-level change. In P. L. Harrison & A. Thomas (Eds.), *Best practices in school psychology: Systems-level services* (pp. 11–28). National Association of School Psychologists.

Center on Positive Behavioral Interventions and Supports. (2020, December). *Positive behavioral interventions and supports (PBIS) evaluation blueprint.* University of Oregon. www.pbis.org.

Chamberlain, P., Brown, C. H., & Saldana, L. (2011). Observational measure of implementation progress in community based settings: The Stages of implementation completion (SIC). *Implementation Science, 6*(116). https://doi.org/10.1186/1748-5908-6-116

Coffey, J., & Horner, R. H. (2012). The sustainability of school-wide positive behavioral interventions and supports. *Exceptional Children, 78*(4), 407–422. https://doi.org/10.1177/001440291207800402

Collaborative for Academic, Social, and Emotional Learning. (2022). *About CASEL.* https://casel.org/about-us/

Collaborative for Academic, Social, and Emotional Learning. (n.d.). *Program guide.* https://pg.casel.org/review-programs/

Data Accountability Center. (2011). *Methods for assessing racial/ ethnic disproportionality in special education: A technical assistance guide (revised).* Westat. www.ideadata.org/docs/RevisedDisproportionality TAguide_FINAL.pdf

Fixsen, D. L., Naoom, S. F., Blasé, K. A., Friedman, R. M., & Wallace, F. (2005). *Implementation research: A synthesis of the literature.* Florida Mental Health Institute, The National Implementation Research Network (FMHI Publication #231).

Flannery, K. B., & McGrath Kato, M. (2017). Implementation of SWPBIS in high school: Why is it different? *Preventing School Failure, 61*(1), 69–79. https://doi.org/10.1080/1045988X.2016.1196644

Gage, N. A., Katsiyannis, A., Carrero, K. M., Miller, R., & Pico, D. (2021). Exploring disproportionate discipline for Latinx students with and without disabilities: A national analysis. *Behavioral Disorders, 46*(1), 1–11. https://doi.org/10.1177/0198742920961356

Han, S. S., & Weiss, B. (2005). Sustainability of teacher implementation of school-based mental health programs. *Journal of Abnormal Child Psychology, 33*(6), 665–679. doi:10.1007/s10802-005-7646-2

Hume, A., & McIntosh, K. (2013). Construct validation of a measure to assess sustainability of school-wide behavior interventions. *Psychology in the Schools, 50*(10), 1003–1014. https://doi.org/10.1002/pits.21722

Kincaid, D., Childs, K., & George, H. (2010). *School-wide benchmarks of quality (revised)*. Unpublished Instrument, University of South Florida.

Kittelman, A., Mercer, S. H., McIntosh, K., & Nese, R. N. T. (2021). Development and validation of a measure assessing sustainability of tier 2 and tier 3 support systems. *Journal of School Psychology*, *85*(4), 140–154. https://doi.org/10.1016/j.jsp.2021.02.001

Latham, G. (1988). The birth and death cycles of educational innovations. *Principal*, *68*(1), 41–43.

Mathews, S., McIntosh, K., Frank, J., & May, S. (2014). Critical features predicting sustained implementation of school-wide positive behavior support. *Journal of Positive Behavior Interventions*, *16*(3), 168–178. http://dx.doi.org/10.1177/1098300713484065

McIntosh, K., Doolittle, J., Vincent, C. G., Horner, R. H., & Ervin, R. A. (2009). *School-wide universal behavior sustainability index: School teams*. The University of British Columbia.

McIntosh, K., Kim, J., Mercer, S. H., Strickland-Cohen, M. K., & Horner, R. H. (2015). Variables associated with enhanced sustainability of school-wide positive behavioral interventions and supports. *Assessment for Effective Intervention*, *40*(3), 184–191. https://doi.org/10.1177/1534508414556503

McIntosh, K., Mercer, S. H., Hume, A. E., Frank, J. L., Turri, M. G., & Mathews, S. (2013). Factors related to sustained implementation of schoolwide positive behavior support. *Exceptional Children*, *79*(3), 293–311. https://doi.org/10.3102/0013189X18776975

McIntosh, K., Mercer, S. H., Nese, R. N. T., Strickland-Cohen, M. K., Kittelman, A., Hoselton, R., & Horner, R. H. (2018). Factors predicting sustained implementation of a universal behavior support framework. *Educational Researcher*, *47*(5), 307–316. https://doi.org/10.3102/0013189X18776975

McIntosh, K., Predy, L. K., Upreti, G., Hume, A. E., Turri, M. G., & Mathews, S. (2014). Perceptions of contextual features related to implementation and sustainability of school-wide positive behavior support. *Journal of Positive Behavior Interventions*, *16*(1), 31–43. https://doi.org/10.1177/1098300712470723

Mcloughlin, C. S., & Noltmeyer, A. L. (2010). Research into factors contributing to discipline use and disproportionality in major urban schools. *Current Issues in Education*, *13*(2). http://cie.asu.edu/.

MissouriSchoolwidePositiveBehaviorSupport.(2020).*2018–2019annual report*. https://assets-global.website-files.com/5d3725188825e071f1670246/5fd3ca38900677828146b514_MI%202018-2019%20SWPBS%20Annual%20Report.pdf

National Implementation Research Network. (2013). *Stages of implementation analysis: Where are we?* National Implementation Research Network, FPG Child Development Institute, University of North Carolina at Chapel Hill.

National Implementation Research Network. (2020). *Implementation stages planning tool*. National Implementation Research Network, FPG Child Development Institute, University of North Carolina at Chapel Hill.

Panzano, P. C., & Roth, D. (2006). The decision to adopt evidence-based and other innovative mental health practices: Risky business? *Psychiatric Services*, *57*(8), 1153–1161. doi:10.1176/ps.2006.57.8.1153

Runge, T. J., Knoster, T. P., Moerer, D., Breinich, T., & Palmiero, J. (2017). A practical protocol for situating mental health evidence-based and promising programs and practices within the Positive behavioral interventions and supports. *Advances in School Mental Health Promotion*, *10*(2), 1–12. https://doi.org/10.1080/1754730X.2017.1285708

Runge, T. J., Staszkiewicz, M. J., Bardo, A. E., Myers, T., Breon, S., & Kozel, M. (2021). *12th annual executive summary of the Pennsylvania positive behavior support network's implementation of school-wide positive behavioral interventions and supports*. Indiana University of Pennsylvania. www.papbs.org

Runge, T. J., Staszkiewicz, M. J., Krouse, J. R., Ulisse, Z. L., Ammerman, K. E., & Hummel, J. (2020). *Summary of the Pennsylvania positive behavior support network's implementation of school-wide positive behavioral interventions and support from 2006–2019*. Indiana University of Pennsylvania.

Skiba, R. J., Peterson, R. L., & Williams, T. (1997). Office referrals and suspension: Disciplinary intervention in middle schools. *Education and Treatment of Children*, *20*(3), 295–313. www.jstor.org/stable/42900491

Skiba, R. J., Poloni-Staudinger, L., Gallini, S., Simmons, A. B., & Feggins-Azziz, R. (2006). Disparate access: The disproportionality of African American students with disabilities across educational environments. *Exceptional Children*, *72*(4), 411–424. https://doi.org/10.1177/001440290607200402

Skiba, R. J., Simmons, A. B., Ritter, S., Gibb, A. C., Rausch, M. K., Cuadrado, J., & Chung, C. (2008). Achieving equity in special education: History, status, and current challenges. *Exceptional Children*, *74*(3), 264–288. https://doi.org/10.1177/001440290807400301

Sugai, G., Horner, R. H., & Lewis-Palmer, T. (2009). *Effective behavior support: Team implementation checklist version 3.0*. Educational and Community Supports.

Sugai, G., Lewis-Palmer, T., Todd, A. W., & Horner, R. H. (2005). *Schoolwide evaluation tool version 2.1*. Educational and Community Supports.

Townsend, B. L. (2000). The disproportionate discipline of African American learners: Reducing school suspensions and expulsions. *Exceptional Children*, *66*(3), 381–391. https://doi.org/10.1177/001440290006600308

Vogt, P. (2005). *Dictionary of statistics and methodology: A nontechnical guide for the social sciences* (3rd ed.). Sage Publications.

Systems-Level PBIS Evaluation Checklist

☐	Establish purpose of the evaluation (e.g., summative, formative, accountability)
☐	Identify key stakeholder groups (e.g., families, students, administrators, educators, community partners)
☐	Select evaluation team members from all stakeholder groups (e.g., expertise, roles on team)
☐	Establish timeline for achieving evaluation process milestones and reporting findings
☐	Define core evaluation questions around five domains: 1. Reach 2. Process 3. Capacity 4. Fidelity 5. Outcomes
☐	Identify evaluation measures/data
☐	Report findings (e.g., written report, presentation)

Note. Checklist created, in part, from National Center on Positive Behavioral Interventions and Supports (2020).

4

Data Rich & Information Rich

The Power of Data

School-based implementation teams have vast amounts of data at their disposal to inform decision-making and evaluate practices. As we saw in the previous chapters, there are data related to perceptions, academics, social-emotional competencies, office discipline referrals, etc. While these data sources are important, the ability to synthesize and action plan around the data remains a difficult task. Despite having access to robust sources and amounts of data, schools often are unable to capitalize on these in a manner that informs actions.

The previous chapters highlighted the importance of equitable data practices, and this chapter seeks to provide recommendations for using the data to execute equity-focused action. Disaggregated data, risk indices and risk ratios offer a look into the types of potential root causes impacting success for specific groups of students. While quantitative information is useful, teams may become overwhelmed or defensive when the data highlight outcomes they did not expect. It is important for the team to engage in establishing meeting agreements for how they will discuss the data and the students themselves. It is also important for teams to seek out "small wins" through intentional goal-setting

DOI: 10.4324/9781003294351-4

and action items. This chapter will highlight root-cause analysis and inquiry as teams.

Much of the information the data provides, whether through disproportionate outcomes or realistic perceptions, is a story that is being told. It is up to the teams to determine how well they will listen and seek to make change. This is also the place where converging data sources along with authentic stakeholder engagement supports any proposed actions. Finally, although there is a focus throughout the book on PBIS implementation, the integration of academic, social, emotional, and behavioral data maximizes opportunities to evaluate current practices and action plan around outcomes indicating minoritized and marginalized students have experienced opportunity gaps.

Using an Equity Mindset to Action Plan

Determining next steps after collecting data can either push teams toward innovative ways of support or simply confirm their expectations, sometimes leading to apathy. Following a specific problem-solving process has the potential to empower school teams to set realistic and achievable goals. Goodman and McIntosh (2016) offered a clear process for problem-solving and action planning: (1) Problem Identification, (2) Problem Clarification, (3) Solution Planning, (4) Goal Setting, (5) Intervention Implementation, and (6) Evaluation. In the previous chapter, the Team Initiated Problem Solving (TIPS) process (Horner et al., 2015) was introduced and operationalizes the problem-solving process in a team structure. Each of the described processes (Table 4.1) highlight the importance of clear identification practices with a focus on solutions, monitoring of progress, and evaluation to make informed decisions for systems and students. Through specific processes and structured agendas, data-based decision-making and action planning is possible and not a sporadic occurrence.

Although the processes previously described the value of problem identification, goal-setting, and solution-focused interventions, root-cause analysis is a must to identify disproportionality for student groups. Root-cause analysis (RCA) is the process of determining the

Table 4.1 Stages of Problem-Solving and TIPS-II processes

Problem-Solving Process McIntosh, K., & Goodman, S. (2016)	TIPS-II Process (Horner et al., 2015)
Problem Identification	*Identify Problem with Precision*
Problem Clarification	*Identify Goal for Change*
Solution Planning	*Identify Solution and Create Implementation Plan with Contextual Fit*
Goal Setting	*Implement Solution with High Integrity*
Intervention Implementation	*Monitor Impact of Solution and Compare Against Goal*
Evaluation	*Make Summative Evaluation Decisions*

foundational causes of the outcomes to establish appropriate systemic approaches for change. "More often than not, an RCA process reveals the systematic nature of how practice and policy gaps can allow the presence of bias-based belief about marginalized populations to operate as a 'rationale' for disproportionate patterns" (Fergus, 2017, pp. 72–73). RCA can be organized into three levels: (1) Outcome Data, (2) Process Data, and (3) Naming the Root Causes (Fergus, 2017). Outcome data describe the intensity, location, and frequency of the outcome pattern. This level of analysis focuses the team's attention on the degree to which equitable outcomes are experienced for all student groups. Process data describe the current practices and policies and how they are executed. This level also allows teams to evaluate where there may be potential gaps in those same policies and practices for supporting all students. Finally, naming the root cause identifies the gap(s) between process data and outcome data. In other words, what are the potential policies that may be intentionally or unintentionally impacting specific student groups in a way that leads to disproportionality? When schools have adopted MTSS/PBIS with fidelity, data-based decisions are based on a process grounded in RCA and consistent monitoring to course-correct as needed. In an ideal system, action planning should be based on this comprehensive approach to data evaluation.

Frameworks such as MTSS and PBIS are often met with criticism when addressing the needs of marginalized and minoritized students. These criticisms speak to practices which continue to neglect the unique assets of students' lived experiences and culturally specific interactions while reinforcing those students who "fit" into the expected behaviors of the dominant culture (Heidelburg et al., 2022; Zakszeski et al., 2021). This rigidity in practice often causes these frameworks to be abandoned or deemed inappropriate for students who are not seen as compliant with norms of the specific educational system. Systems may include county-level, district-level, or building-level policies and practices. While these criticisms are valid, given the experiences of those who have witnessed frameworks attempted without fidelity or without culturally responsive practices at their core, it is important to know that the frameworks themselves are only as effective as those who implement them. Implementation drivers (Bertram et al., 2014), who typically originate at the MTSS/PBIS team level, are the immediate people who drive policies and influence practice.

An equity mindset suggests adopting a perspective which poses questions to ensure that those students, no matter their race, ethnicity, religion, gender identity, sexual orientation, disability status, or family income, have access, opportunity, and inclusion as part of the fabric of the school or district setting. This mindset also speaks to an openness in considering whether the produced outcomes in the data sets are not solely based on the individual student or student group. The willingness to examine the structures which may be impacting the outcomes is a necessary step in the process of adopting an equitable mindset. While structural examination is critical, individual reflection is the most important exercise to develop a mindset focused on equity, inclusion, and belonging. While many speak to adopting an equity lens, a mindset is not something that can be applied when it is convenient or when the situation requires it. A mindset speaks to consistently applying skills and perspectives that foster growth and cultural humility.

What is Self & System Awareness?

Consider a time when you were meeting someone for the first time; you hear their last name, see their head covering or their attire, and determine that they must not be originally from America. As you begin the conversation, you proceed to ask them where they are from, and they respond that they are from Chicago, Illinois. Taken aback, you ask, "Where are you really from?" The person looks perturbed and proceeds to repeat that they are from Chicago, and you notice the conversation abruptly changes. In this example, an individual interaction demonstrated many social concepts that impact how we show up to others and how others show up to us.

In another example, consider your team reviewing disciplinary data. In the meeting, there is discussion around the office discipline referral information for the month. A team member notes an increase in defiant behavior among fifth graders in the hallway around dismissal at 3:00 pm. The perceived motivation appears to be peer attention. Another team member asks for the names of the students who are making up the majority of the data for that precise problem statement. A review of the students shows more female than male students. Another team member says, "Oh, I know those girls . . . they are from Miss Smith's class, and you know that's the emotional support room." The team collectively says, "Ohhhhh . . . ." Someone says, "I don't think we should spend too much time during this meeting trying to problem-solve around this data, because those students already have IEPs (individualized education programs), and their behaviors are pretty consistent. What can we really do about it?" This example also demonstrates many social concepts that impact how we show up to others and how others show up to us.

In both examples, there is a lack of self and system awareness. Self-awareness is the ability to have a reflective consciousness of how you understand the impact of your implicit thoughts, feelings, and behaviors (Eurich, 2018). We define *system awareness* as taking the reflective approach described through the self-awareness process when considering impact and expanding to the evaluation of the system as it relates to intended outcomes. While intentions may be sincere, the impact of how you react, respond, and act has ramifications for the stability of a relationship or an outcome. In both cases, the impact of words led to actions that ultimately may cause harm. In the example of the one-on-one conversation, the person who was asked about their country of origin experienced a microaggression. In the second example, the school-based team held low expectations of the students they were discussing and determined that the data pointed to a student-level issue without ownership from the team on how to innovate potential interventions of support.

System and self-awareness are processes that often begin with unpacking who we are and what we represent. Identity is a concept that often influences how we interpret or relate to others, whether there are shared identities or if there are vastly divergent identity experiences. Social identities are those pieces of ourselves which impact how we view others, who and what we value, where we find commonality and understanding, and who we see as different. Those who are seen as different may also be viewed with a deficit-mindset, dependent upon our preconceived view of their backgrounds or our stereotypes. Social identities may include the following:

- ◆ National Origin
- ◆ Ethnicity
- ◆ Race
- ◆ Age
- ◆ Ability Status
- ◆ Religion/Spirituality
- ◆ Sexual Orientation
- ◆ Gender Identity

A 41-year-old, able-bodied, Christian, cisgender, heterosexual female, who identifies as a Black American, with an ethnicity from West Africa and Northwestern Europe, captures one of the author's social identities. It should be noted that the clarity around ethnicity and other identities is not a simple process. For example, some Black Americans, as descendants of the African diaspora, may have difficulty identifying their ethnicity. In some cases, family history is passed down, or genetic testing offers helpful information. Another author may complete this process by identifying as a nearly 50-year-old, White, Protestant, heterosexual male, of German American heritage, raised by a Lutheran pastor and mother. While these two individuals share some commonalities, their unique identities influence how they view the world, how others view them, and what society may view as more valued. Both may have similar views around politics, religion, or sexuality; however, at face value, their visible identities may impact how each author navigates specific situations where their identities may be singularly connected to a stereotype. When this occurs, either one of the authors may wish to shed one of their identities in order to fit in. This level of self-awareness offers a glimpse into others' lived experiences and how they may not experience a sense of belonging on a consistent basis.

In many school districts, professional learning with an equity focus may begin with an exercise around unpacking these social identities. The Social Identity Wheel (University of Michigan, 2021) is one of the activities which helps participants discuss their identities, consider which identities we are most aware of, which identities would be easy to give away, or which identities would be impossible to release no matter the circumstances. Often this process can be enlightening for some and uncomfortable for others. When this exercise has been observed by a facilitator, there are often a range of emotions; however, the goal of the process is to help each person consider how their social identities may impact how they view others and how these identities influence their positionality, professionally and personally. In some cases, participants may adamantly refuse to "give away" any of their identities and some have expressed offense by being asked to do so. The goal of the process is to consider how others are often asked to shed identities in order to assimilate into environments, where one or more of their identities may not be honored or deemed appropriate.

For some, an exercise similar to what has been described may feel invasive by the school team; however, when done with appropriate facilitation, this exercise and others like it are helpful for teams to improve their self-awareness and thereby improve their ability to evaluate data with an equitable, inclusive, and belonging mindset. Henri Tajfel and Turner (1979) described Social Identity Theory as the ways a person sees themselves and how their group membership offers them a sense of belonging. Three stages of the Social Identity Theory are noted

Figure 4.1 Three processes of Social Identity Theory
Adapted from: Tajfel, H., & Turner, J. C. (1979). An Integrative Theory of Intergroup Conflict. In W. G. Austin, & S. Worchel (Eds.), *The Social Psychology of Intergroup Relations* (pp. 33–47). Monterey, CA: Brooks/Cole.

in Figure 4.1. Each stage offers an explanation to describe how easily social identity can contribute to how biases are shaped and ultimately may manifest in deficit thinking and data-based decision-making.

What is Implicit Bias?

Consider the two examples offered at the onset of this discussion. In one instance, a microaggression occurred and in the other, expectations were established based on preconceived notions regarding ability. The concept of implicit or unconscious bias was most likely at the root of both situations. Implicit bias has commonly been defined as "the attitudes or stereotypes that affect our understanding, actions, and decisions in an unconscious manner" (The Kirwan Institute, 2012, para. 1). This should not be considered a replacement or rationale for explicit bias, which is a clear and blatant expression of discrimination or harassment. Considering Social Identity Theory and the final stage of social comparison, this is where people generally associate certain characteristics, experiences, and language with a social group. These associations may be influenced by what is seen on television, social media, or from our family discussions. Our brains are wired for associations, and can sometimes take shortcuts to make quick decisions and actions (Benson & Fiarman, 2019). In many cases, we, as humans, are unaware that these biases are influencing our thoughts and may even experience dissonance upon realizing bias was instrumental in our decision-making and action planning.

As school teams, you may ask, how do we address individual thoughts, feelings, and behaviors? How do we know that we have engaged in microaggressions or have biases? How are we supposed to change how people view others? Is that our role? These are heavy questions and may seem impossible to address. While each team dynamic presents its own unique context, there are some considerations to ensure a team is able to lean into discomfort to achieve a level of functionality where teammates are affirmed, voices are valued, and disagreement is healthy. Transferred power on a school-based team is one way to ensure healthy interactions. "It means shared power and ownership in who the team is and the work the team does. It requires that power be used equitably, humanely, for the right purposes, in the right ways, and toward, the right ends" (Radd et al., 2021, p. 131). To embrace this type of teaming structure, professional learning is a critical component which develops team members both personally and professionally as they evaluate data and consider each of the concepts outlined earlier from their own social identity to unpacking their own implicit biases. At the conclusion of this chapter, there is a sample professional learning series to support teams as they develop an equity mindset.

The sample professional learning series offers a variety of potential topics and are provided in a way to unpack identity, implicit bias, and the recognition of inequities. While each of the sample topics provide a specific focus, the core theme of the series is to build awareness, understanding, and action across building-based teams. Adopting an equity mindset or any paradigm shift requires thoughtful development and planning. Professional learning is a mechanism to engage in that development process and begin the necessary steps toward change. It is not enough to offer professional development in educational settings at one faculty meeting. Expecting sustainable change from a one-time professional development offering is unrealistic and may inadvertently perpetuate a sense of compliance rather than authentic engagement. The sample series offers a training plan dedicated to each of the teams in the school building. Following a structure typically seen using the MTSS framework, core teams, advanced tiered teams, grade-level teams, and full faculty engage in learning offerings that are tailored to their role/function. This allows for each team to have a connection but ensures that capacity is being built to cascade information across teams. Various teams in a school building serve a function, but without a cohesive approach, these teams may become siloed and singularly driven around their own needs and goals.

The authors have experienced supporting PBIS teams where there is hesitancy around the best approach to professional learning. Often this is rooted in finding time, fear of overwhelming or alienating staff, or simply being unsure of whether the information will transfer into practice. Couple these challenges with content that may be viewed as controversial, difficult to initially measure, and steeped in deep-rooted beliefs. The sample training series offers a differentiated approach to process through consultation and coaching of evaluating data at the various team levels. In addition, the full faculty is engaged in learning that is more introductory and allows for continued growth. This often allows each team or group the opportunity to participate through a particular entry point. These entry points consider roles, responsibilities, and developed understanding of systems-level change. Safir and Dugan (2021) described the importance of avoiding the trap of siloing equity. They identified this as isolating work around equitable practices to one team, one plan, or even one person. For the purposes of this text, the authors describe the sample training series beginning with the core PBIS team. Throughout the sample, the advanced tiers team, grade-level teams, and full faculty are delineated as part of an intentional cascade approach to professional learning. The goal of developing a differentiated approach to professional learning in this sample is to build capacity across multiple teams, reduce siloing, and promote sustainability across time.

Core PBIS teams are often tasked with evaluating the health of the universal practices across the system. They are often responsible for ensuring and promoting understanding of PBIS, evaluating disciplinary and climate data, action planning around the data discussions, and continuously monitoring and course correcting through the implementation process. Often they are considered the frontline of information and dissemination of strategies to the other respective members of the school system. As a core team, there is a significant need for continuous learning and growth to ensure there is ongoing drive for innovative and sustainable approaches. If the core team has engaged in foundational professional learning around PBIS and has established initial structures to inform systems, data, and practices, the next steps of detecting disproportionality and evaluating if the climate is positive for every learner would be a needed progression. The sample professional learning series describes the month of August as a time where the core team is beginning to disaggregate office discipline referrals and gain insight on which student groups may be experiencing disproportionate outcomes. For example, the team may evaluate their office discipline referrals and notice that there are a high number of students using inappropriate language in the hallways around 2:30 pm and the perceived motivation is peer attention. When the team is able to disaggregate this problem statement, they notice certain student groups are making up most of the referrals at this time (e.g., Latino/x males in sixth grade). The core team would probably not have noticed this trend without disaggregating the data.

While the action for the core team does not stop at identification, this is the progression of professional learning that has the ability to impact (1) how the team conducts their data analysis, (2) what questions they will pose to ensure they are being equitable in implementation, and (3) how they will approach the staff, families, and communities to mitigate disproportionate outcomes. This initial shift in practice will be uncomfortable for some and may cause team members to question their own beliefs and thoughts as the data tells a story that may be hard to hear. The next phase of the sample professional learning series asks the core team to establish meeting agreements and allow the team to come to consensus on their relational interactions during meetings. This should not be a rushed process. Skilled facilitators will often provide the team with sample agreements and then allow the team to determine and add those that seem most appropriate for the team's overall role and function. The following section will describe how to apply these efforts and shift from simply reviewing numbers and graphs to actively listening to the data story and creating equitable action.

Moving From Numbers to Sense

As teams begin to analyze data sources, particularly discipline and climate data in the PBIS framework, simply knowing the numbers is not enough for actionable change. An ability to engage in an intentional process for determining the impact of current practices is contingent upon the team's willingness to trust each other, experience difficult dialogue, remain committed to the outlined goals, and understand that this process is continuous. Given the aforementioned process of self-awareness, each team member is approaching the work with a varied experience and perspective. Terms of engagement are valuable for the team to experience success when navigating difficult discussions. Developing agreements as a team is a way to establish how members plan to hold each other accountable for ensuring a psychologically safe space.

Glenn Singleton (2015) described courageous conversations about race as having four agreements: (1) Stay engaged, (2) Speak your truth, (3) Experience discomfort, and (4) Expect and accept non-closure. Though Singleton's focus was around the construct of race, these agreements are applicable for brave conversations about socioeconomic status, religion, ability, gender identity, sexual orientation, and language. Additionally, using the term agreements provides the opportunity for those who are typically marginalized, minoritized, or excluded to have some say in the development and adoption of the agreements. Establishing group norms has the potential to create a process where what is considered "normal" is how the team will engage. Other agreements to consider when operating with an equity mindset may include: (1) go slow to go fast, (2) consider your intent and the potential impact, and (3) exercise forgiveness. There are many examples of team agreements to consider, however finding three to five would be ideal in an effort to commit them to memory and make them a part of the fabric of the meeting structure.

Upon establishing team agreements, it will be important to level-set around universal language and understanding. When considering definitions of equity, inclusion, diversity, and belonging there are a variety of ways to describe these terms. In many cases, these definitions are formed through social identities, group membership, past experiences, and core values. In prior experiences, seeking a foundational definition of equity that fits the context of the system would be important. Prior to adopting a definition for any of these key terms, there are questions to consider to ensure foundational understanding is obtained and can be applied across processes and policies. These questions may include: What should equity look like, sound like, and feel like in our system? Are students getting what they need to be successful, instead of everyone getting the same thing (equity vs. equality)? How do we view inclusion? What is a sense of belonging for our students, families, and staff? Are we diverse in thoughts and in backgrounds? Once these questions are considered, being clear about how the team is defining these terms coupled with the established agreements can serve as anchors for the team as they engage in action planning.

Earlier in this chapter, action planning with an equity mindset was described as engaging in self-awareness, establishing a psychologically safe space for analysis, and determining action steps that will seek to eliminate disproportionate outcomes for marginalized and minoritized students. The Austin Independent School District (2020) created a process for equity-focused decision-making in an effort to ensure action planning is done through the mindset of equity, inclusion, and belonging. In the initial step, teams are asked to consider who is at the "decision-making table." Is it the same group of staff members who always volunteer for school-based teams? Is there the opportunity for diversity of thoughts or opinions? Who is not being heard? What terms of engagement are deemed acceptable and are other methods welcomed?

Once those questions are considered, the next step speaks to the needs or problems the team is looking to address. Key questions in this step include: Which groups are historically impacted by the current policies and practices? What is our timeline to make changes? Whose experiences should be centered in this process? Once the actions are proposed and implemented, are the solutions working for those who were identified as being most impacted? Mascaranaz (2022) suggested "getting proximate" with those who have historically been impacted by systemic policies and practices. This means communicating directly with them and not simply assuming that this solution will be best for them. Lastly, how will we hold ourselves accountable by monitoring progress of the solution? Communication of current progress will be critical, along with the willingness to consider alternative pathways if the progress is minimal.

The process just described is a sound approach for a team to focus on equity in decision-making. As a school-based team, the theme of engaging students, families, and communities is woven into this practice. It is not enough to survey students, families, and other vested partners. Authentic engagement would allow for their voices to be valued in overall decision-making and action planning experiences. It would be unfair to assume that each caregiver has the ability to sit in on a team meeting or feel comfortable offering input. In another example of self and system awareness, the team has to consider how historically marginalized or minoritized families have typically interfaced with schools. There may be cultural considerations for some families in how they view the school system, or there previously may have been poor experiences when they were students themselves or past experiences as a caregiver advocating for their child. In some cases, students and families may have been asked to serve on a team only to find that their presence was there for the sake of appearances or the conversation was filled with jargon, and they were unable to meaningfully participate. Lisa Delpit (1995) described the concept of "silenced dialogue" where traditionally marginalized or minoritized individuals participate in discussions silently, as they may feel as though their voice or experience may be dismissed or invalidated.

A school team may wonder, "How are we supposed to know if silenced dialogue is happening?" The team might think, "That parent did not object when we recommended that intervention. What are we supposed to do?" Unfortunately, the *silence* may imply agreement and create a situation where the team adds to an action plan and finds that the strategy fails or there is significant resistance from the community it was intended to support. Aside from considering the equity decision-making process previously described, school teams may consider engaging with *cultural brokers*. Cultural brokers are defined as

> Individuals who act as bridges between schools and diverse families. These school staff, community-based personnel, or

volunteers typically: 1. educate parents to support the school's goals to improve student achievement; 2. connect parents to resources and information; and 3. advocate with parents and with school staff to promote change or decrease conflict.

(Torres et al., 2015, p. 2)

Cultural brokers may serve as a valuable resource to ensure the team is responsive and responsible to the students and communities it serves. It is impossible to have all of the answers or the insight to understand each nuance of every single culture represented in your system. Also, it would be presumptuous to assume that each culture is a monolith. This humility in understanding others and engaging in intentional listening and learning is a pivotal practice.

The authors have experienced consulting with teams where the need for a cultural broker would have created an improved approach to supporting students. In one example, one of the authors was consulting with a core PBIS team at the elementary level. The school building housed over 400 students, in addition over 27 various languages were spoken. The diversity of the building was viewed by the community and staff as a strength and something that made the building unique. During the school's third year of implementation of PBIS, they noticed an increase of a particular ethnic group in their student body. A number of teachers reported several students who were new to the school arriving at school with weather-worn shoes. They expressed concern to the principal and requested to hold a shoe drive to collect shoes to provide to the students and families in perceived need. The principal tasked the leadership team of the building, which served as an MTSS/PBIS team, to organize the drive, determine a dissemination plan, and ensure the students with perceived need were able to access the new shoes first. Overall, the shoe drive was a success, and there were plenty of new shoes to share with families and students. The staff provided the shoes to the families and were thrilled that they had come together as a school community to support their students.

The following week, teachers reported the students who had worn the tattered shoes were still arriving at school in the same condition. The leadership team was puzzled and thought they had covered everything with regards to shoe sizes, selected families, etc. One of the teachers on the leadership team mentioned that there was a local pastor who was connected to many of the families who represented the ethnic group, and he wondered if the pastor may be able to offer some insight. The team invited the pastor to their next meeting, detailed their intention around the shoe drive, and wondered why the students were not wearing the shoes that were donated. The pastor explained that in their culture it is viewed as disrespectful to accept *handouts* and that the families held high levels of pride and did not understand why they were given the shoes without an explanation from the school. In this example, the pastor served as a cultural broker, who provided valuable information on how the team could have considered their approach to become more responsive to the cultures they were serving.

Similar to effectively engaging families and leveraging cultural brokers, authentic student engagement is more than asking students or families to complete a survey. Students hold the information on what works best for them. Safir and Dugan (2021) described the importance of avoiding transactional listening, a type of listening without the intent of valuing the information they share, becoming defensive when offered feedback, or appearing disinterested as they describe their experiences. Nonverbal communication is loud, and students are very astute in knowing if a person is genuinely interested in them. This can also apply to student participation on a school-based team. Their presence is the minimum requirement for involvement. Engagement would lend itself to having voice, valuing the voice, and actively applying their recommendations.

One way student voice would be valuable would be in the development and delivery of acknowledgment systems. A key component of PBIS implementation is the consistent and appropriate use of acknowledgments to create and sustain positive school climate and connection. In some cases, these acknowledgment systems can bring their own share of inequity, depending upon the buy-in from staff, frequency, context, and which students are in receipt of the acknowledgments. Acknowledgment systems are often the source of pushback from staff and families that "PBIS is just about rewards." This creates a need for core teams to ensure the acknowledgment system is applied in a manner that is sensible and tied directly to expectations. Additionally, the acknowledgment system should be monitored to ensure the same students are not the only participants able to access tangibles or opportunities. This often takes time on the part of staff who are disseminating acknowledgments by way of a resistance to providing acknowledgments to the students they often see as meeting expectations and intentionally seeking out those who are usually not considered when they recognize situationally appropriate behavior.

Teams may begin to notice the acknowledgments they selected for the system are losing their popularity. They may wonder if they should change the acknowledgment system and begin to prototype other team-based recommendations. This continued cycle of course correction, without the input of the students, families, or communities, can become futile and may stifle the implementation efforts of PBIS. It is important to remember that the PBIS framework is based upon drivers of change. Students are able to articulate the acknowledgments that motivate them to remain connected to the school community. For example, a team may suggest lunch with the principal as an acknowledgment and students may disagree with that option and prefer lunch with the school counselor or with their teacher. Without gathering student input, the team may have maintained the original lunch option and saw the participation or motivation for students to seek out the acknowledgment dwindle. If the acknowledgments are not serving as a motivator, it is also possible for an increase in office discipline referrals. Teams, who are beginning to move from numbers to sense, may begin embedding key questions in team meetings with regard to the health of the acknowledgment system. These may include:

◆ Per grade-level/department, how many acknowledgments have been distributed across the month?
◆ Among the grade levels/departments, which students or student groups are not receiving the same level of acknowledgments? Can we hypothesize why not?
◆ How do we know the acknowledgments are appropriate? Are students reporting positive experiences? Have we checked in with families as well?

◆ Do we need to adjust any part of the acknowledgment system to provide access to more students?

◆ How are our staff acknowledgments being received? Have we checked in with the staff to see if we could do something different?

Checklists have been provided at the conclusion of this chapter for teams to consider as they develop and refine acknowledgment systems for students and for staff.

Each of the previously described practices for teams to move from numbers to sense are leaning into the human experience of the generated solutions. The numbers tell one part of a story; however, the students, families, and communities connected to the data offer school teams the genuine opportunity to build a sustainable positive school climate. While this book focuses on equitable practices in PBIS, it is imperative for these considerations to apply across educational domains, specifically academics, social-emotional learning, mental wellness, and behavior.

Integration of Academics, SEL, Mental Wellness, and PBIS

The recommended practices for becoming data rich and information rich apply to more than just equitable PBIS practices. For true sustainability of a framework like MTSS or PBIS, integrated approaches are necessary. Operating in silos is often the easiest way to stifle implementation efforts and overwhelm a system. Chapter 2 offered a plethora of data sources for teams to ensure they are able to integrate their systems across domains. However, McIntosh and Goodman (2016) highlighted the importance of not integrating systems, teams, data, and practices simply for the sake of integrating. Purposeful integration of academics, social-emotional learning (SEL), mental wellness, and PBIS is a pathway to maintaining successful implementation practices and improved outcomes. For example, considering social identity, implicit bias, and using an equity mindset to evaluate data crosses multiple areas. A way to consider how to ensure equitable practices are happening across the system would be to evaluate and consider potential ways decision-making may be impacting results. Snap decisions, for example, could not only influence behavioral consequences but also participation in extracurricular activities, recommendations for gifted screening, recommendations for additional intervention, or willingness to engage authentically with families. The following information offers a way to identify and potentially mitigate snap decisions. This is provided within the context of disciplinary decisions that influence disproportionality.

Vulnerable decision points (VDPs) occur in a "given situation coupled with a person's internal state that increases the likelihood of bias affecting discipline decision making" (Cave, 2019, para. 1). Traditionally, VDPs are contextualized around emotional states that impact a person's reaction to a trigger. When evaluating behavioral data, school teams may be able to determine if a pattern of office discipline referrals may be at a specific time of the day, location, or day of the week. In some cases, teams are able to evaluate if there is a specific subset of staff or one staff member who typically issues the disciplinary referral and to specific groups of students. This will be described in the accompanying vignette.

Concepts like VDPs and neutralizing routines are not typically concepts or skills used by most educational staff. We may be aware that we make quick decisions each day but may not have the awareness of how to slow the process or recognize triggers for our response. The information and understanding needed is best provided through professional learning and coaching. When considering the sample professional learning plan provided in this chapter, there are sessions dedicated to the concept of VDPs and neutralizing routines. After introducing disaggregated disciplinary data to the team, delivery of content around equity and disproportionality, and the establishment of meeting agreements, the core team is asked to evaluate their social identities. As previously described, this process allows the team to engage in the self-awareness journey and consider how their particular identities may influence how they view behaviors, expectations, and those with different lived experiences. While the social identity process is ongoing, it foundationally primes the team for the next learning session which introduces VDPs and neutralizing routines.

During this time, participants are provided with examples of decision-states such as hunger and fatigue. The authors have found that beginning with physical states may serve as an entry-point for team members to connect and see how VDPs could happen to anyone. This reduces immediate discomfort or defensiveness when considering their own decision-making. These types of decisions happen all day and may occur both personally and professionally. From there, examples are offered that represent student interactions or behaviors such as disrespect, defiance, disruption, or inappropriate language. These types of behaviors are often considered subjective in nature, as what may be seen as disrespectful or defiant to one person may not have the same impact for another person (McIntosh, 2014). The ambiguity of these types of behaviors may lead to variable responses and reactions that may be rooted in a person's lived experience, their family values, beliefs, and ideals. As the professional learning continues, there are other examples provided, such as prior experiences with the student or family. For instance, if a teacher has taught a number of students from the same family and has had difficult interactions in the past with those family members, it is possible that they have already determined how they will navigate the new school year when the younger sibling arrives in their classroom. They may not consciously expect problematic behavior, but when any behavior (even mild) occurs, a VDP might occur and adversely influence their decision-making toward discipline VDP.

VDPs are identified most easily through data analysis. As humans, we often lack awareness of how we engage in quick decision-making processes. Our brains are wired for associations, and we often resort to fast and succinct ways of completing tasks or escaping an unwanted experience. Through data dives, teams are able to begin the process of uncovering potential VDPs that may be influencing outcomes. As teams evaluate their tier 1 data at monthly meetings and create precise problem-statements, their student management systems may have the capability to further explain potential root causes. For example, if eighth grade students are receiving multiple office referrals during Miss Hamilton's language arts class for disruption, the need to determine if there are other contributing factors may be necessary. In other tier 1 data, the team may have found that female students are receiving more referrals than males across the system. When specifically focusing on the data in Miss Hamilton's class, more than half of her referrals are for female students. When the core team representative from that grade-level team discussed the data with Miss Hamilton, she indicated that the *"girls were really giving her a hard time."* She noted that they seemed to finish their work quickly, and she did not believe they were actually taking the work seriously. She said they were often disruptive and complained of boredom. The core team representative asked if Miss Hamilton had seen the latest literacy screening data and pointed out that the same students who were receiving office discipline referrals were performing well on the reading assessment. Miss Hamilton said it really bothered her that the girls said they were bored because she was trying her best to make the classroom instruction engaging. She agreed that she would often lose her temper when she heard them complain because she was doing her best and could not figure out what she could be doing wrong. Additionally, she had been warned by other teachers that the eighth grade female students often challenged newer teachers. In this example, Miss Hamilton's VDP was frustration over perceived criticism of her teaching skills and the expectation that the female students were deliberately being difficult toward her.

Once a VDP is identified, either through conferencing with the staff members or through hypothesizing with the team, the creation of a neutralizing routine to mitigate the VDP would be recommended. Neutralizing routines are "an instructional response to unwanted behavior instead of a harsher one. It is a quick, clear, doable action that interrupts the chain of events and keeps students involved in instruction" (Cave, 2019, para. 1). These routines take practice and accountability from others, with the understanding that each of us have biases, and even if our VDPs are different, being able to serve as a partner to your colleague is necessary for these routines to become just that: routine.

Let us return to the example of Miss Hamilton and her language arts class. Now that the VDP has been identified, the core team representative offered to meet and discuss creating a neutralizing routine.

Miss Hamilton noted that at home when she is feeling overwhelmed or quick-tempered, she will write herself a quick note telling herself to stop and breathe. The core team representative suggested she try this routine for a week and see if there was any difference in how she responds to the female students in her class. Miss Hamilton also discussed how she was planning to evaluate how she could provide more challenging opportunities for the students who were expressing boredom with the content. After a week, the core team representative checked in with Miss Hamilton. She reported that it was difficult at first to remember her note routine, but she is willing to keep trying. She also said she sat down with the female students and asked them why they felt bored in her class. The students said they felt like they already knew the concepts and felt held back when Miss Hamilton forced them to do *busy-work*. Miss Hamilton explained that she has a variety of students in the classroom, who are each doing their best and now that she is aware of their concerns, she would do her best to make sure they were challenged. Miss Hamilton said she would keep the core team representative posted and appreciated the support. While this example appears easy, the process of identifying VDPs and neutralizing routines are not always so clear. Teams will need to ensure they have a clear understanding of how to detect VDPs and then have the ability to recommend or coach others in the development of neutralizing routines that are contextually appropriate.

Vulnerable decision points and the need for neutralizing routines (McIntosh, 2014) are not exclusive to disciplinary decisions. As school teams evaluate academic data, social-emotional competencies, and mental wellness, there is a need to determine if implicit bias is manifested in decisions made by staff or by the interventions/actions established by school teams. It is easy to view academic data, social-emotional learning, and mental wellness with a lens of bias. The defensiveness that may occur when data are evaluated and points toward the system rather than the student is an example of a systemic VDP. Having the ability to engage in a team-based neutralizing routine to shift deficit-based thinking around academic gaps, opportunity losses, social-emotional difficulties, and mental wellness challenges allows for system shifts instead of student/family and community blame. This is especially important if a team is seeking to embed equitable practices across a system of support. The variety of data sources (academic, behavioral, social-emotional) offer an important story, and once the data is analyzed, the action steps necessary cannot operate in a vacuum. A comprehensive approach to ensuring every student has access and opportunity to experience belonging is contingent on how an integrated framework exists to drive the system.

Conclusion

An *information-rich* school-based team has the ability to transform the school's foundation into one that is solidly rooted in radical inclusion (Ortiz Guzman, 2017). This type of inclusion honors the stories, experiences, feedback, and assets of those being served. As we've noted, data tell a story, and it is up to the team evaluating the data to decide if they are willing to listen and act.

Now that we have discussed data analysis, action planning and professional learning, how can those foundational tenets translate into practice? What creates the conditions for sustainability of practice? MTSS/PBIS teams are in a pivotal position to understand the purpose of their journey, how to enhance their practices along the way, and how the work can become foundationally *business as usual*. Understanding how to establish foundational practices, as outlined in the previous and current chapters, offers guideposts for teams embarking on their journey. The next stop will extend the pathway toward effective practices with the goal of impacting outcomes. See you there!

Chapter 4: Seeds for Growth

◆ Much of the information the data provides, whether through disproportionate outcomes or realistic perceptions, indicate there is a **story that is being told**. It is up to the teams to determine how well they will listen and seek to make change.

- **Root-cause analysis** is the process of determining the foundational causes of the outcomes to determine appropriate systemic approaches for change.
- An equity mindset suggests **adopting a perspective** which poses questions to ensure that those students, no matter their race, ethnicity, religion, gender identity, sexual orientation, or family income, have **access, opportunity**, and **inclusion as part of the fabric of the school or district setting**. This mindset also speaks to an openness in considering the produced outcomes in the data sets are not solely based on the individual student or student group.
- **Professional learning** is a critical component which develops team members both personally and professionally as they evaluate data and consider their own social identity and unpack their own implicit biases.
- **Purposeful integration** of academics, social-emotional learning, mental wellness, and PBIS is a pathway to maintaining successful implementation and improved outcomes. For example, considering social identity, implicit bias, and using an equity mindset to evaluate data **crosses domains**.

Vignette/Example

The vignette that follows describes a team that has begun their journey of data analysis and the need for an adopted equity mindset to engage in a process that requires more than problem identification but rather root-cause analysis and inquiry. Disproportionate data can be overwhelming to teams. It is important to remember that "approaching these problems as if these are static factors can lead to apathy, rather than empowerment" (Hyson et al., 2020, p. 53). Teams must remain vigilant and committed to their goals of ensuring positive school climates for all students and honoring their unique characteristics, which may be impacting their ability to thrive in the system.

Gonzala Elementary School (fictitious school name) is considered a suburban school, with 625 students, grades K–5. Gonzala has been

Table 4.2 Demographic characteristics of Gonzala Elementary School

Characteristic	Proportion of Student Population
Asian	13.6%
Black/African American	24.5%
Hispanic/Latino/a/x	8.2%
White	45.0%
Multi-Racial	8.6%
Economically Disadvantaged	46.4%
English Learner	11.4%
Foster Care	0.3%
Homeless	1.1%

engaged in the PBIS framework for at least 3 years and has received statewide recognition of implementation with fidelity at tier 1. Their demographics are as follows:

The principal at Gonzala, Mrs. Book, has been attending statewide training around equity in discipline and how schools implementing PBIS should be evaluating data related to disproportionality through risk indices and risk ratios. When Mrs. Book considered the landscape of her school, she initially wondered if her team needed to do this type of analysis as she was certain that their discipline referrals were being doled out fairly. Mrs. Book wanted more information, however, and decided to reach out to their PBIS district coach to see if they would be willing to *run the numbers*. The district coach was able to complete the analysis and found the following risk ratios: Black/African American–2.7; White–1.2; Asian–0.5; Hispanic/Latino/a/x–1.7; Multi-Racial–2.0.

Mrs. Book was shocked and immediately called her team together to review the data and attempt to problem-solve how to reduce these disproportionate outcomes. She learned that a risk ratio higher than 1.0 indicated overrepresentation, and she was especially concerned about the data for Black/African American and Multi-Racial students. To Mrs. Book's chagrin, the team was mixed in their reactions to the data. Some offered that the students who identified as

Black/African American or Multi-Racial typically came from homes where education was not valued, and their behaviors reflected what their parents tolerated. Others seemed genuinely dismayed by the data and wondered how these numbers were accurate and what they could do differently. Mrs. Book recalled in her training around equity and discipline that it may be important to support her team in professional learning around setting agreements for how they will engage in data dialogue with an equity mindset, identifying VDPs, and creating neutralizing routines. She knew that having this foundational learning would be useful as the team would need to dig deeper into the data to determine the type of infractions students were receiving, what time of day, by whom, and the location. She had a hypothesis that the top reason for referral for students who identified as Black/African American and Multi-Racial was for disrespect. She had learned that this was a highly subjective behavior and would be potentially influenced by implicit bias. Mrs. Book consulted with her district coach to determine an appropriate professional learning sequence for her team and apply those skills in their upcoming meetings and data analysis.

References

Austin Independent School District. (2020). *Equity-Focused decision making level #1.* www.austinisd.org/sites/default/files/dept/equity-office/docs/Equity-Focused-Decision-Making.pdf

Benson, T. A., & Fiarman, S. E. (2019). *Unconscious bias in schools: A developmental approach to exploring race and racism.* Harvard Education Press.

Bertram, R. M., Blase, K. A., & Fixsen, D. L. (2014). Improving programs and outcomes: Implementation frameworks and organization change. *Research on Social Work Practice, 25*(4), 477–487. https://doi.org/10.1177%2F1049731514537687

Cave, M. (2019, November 12). *Don't discipline hangry: 3 steps to a better classroom.* PBIS Apps. www.pbisapps.org/articles/dont-discipline-hangry-3-steps-to-a-better-classroom

Delpit. (1995b). The silenced dialogue. In L. Delpit (Ed.), *Other people's children: Cultural conflict in the classroom* (pp. 21–47). The New Press. (Original work published 1988)

Eurich, T. (2018). *What self awareness really is and how to cultivate it.* https://hbr.org/2018/01/what-self-awareness-really-is-and-how-to-cultivate-it

Fergus, E. (2017). *Solving disproportionality and achieving equity: A leader's guide to using data to change hearts and minds.* Corwin.

Heidelburg, K., Rutherford, L., & Parks, T. W. (2022). A preliminary analysis assessing SWPBIS implementation fidelity in relation to disciplinary outcomes of black students in urban schools. *The Urban Review, 54*(3), 138–154 https://doi.org/10.1007/s11256-021-00609

Horner, R. H., Newton, J. S., Todd, A. W., Algozzine, B., Algozzine, K., Cusumano, D. L., & Preston, A. I. (2015). *The team-initiated problem solving (TIPS II) training materials.* www.TIPS2info.blogspot.com.

Hyson, D. M., Kovaleski, J. F., Silberglitt, B., & Pedersen, J. A. (2020). *The data-driven school: Collaborating to improve student outcomes. The Guilford practical intervention in the schools series.* Guilford.

The Kirwan Institute. (2012). *Understanding implicit bias.* https://kirwaninstitute.osu.edu/article/understanding-implicit-bias

Mascaranaz, L. (2022). *Evident equity: A guide for creating systemwide change in schools.* Solution Tree Press.

McIntosh, K., Girvan, E., Horner, R., & Smolkowski, K. (2014). Education not incarceration: A conceptual model for reducing racial and ethnic disproportionality in school discipline. *Journal of Applied Research on Children: Informing Policy for Children at Risk, 5*(2), Article 4.

McIntosh, K., & Goodman, S. (2016). *Integrated multi-tiered systems of support: Blending RTI and PBIS.* Guilford.

Ortiz Guzman, C. M. (2017). *Equity design: Leveraging identity development in the creation of an anti-racist equitable design thinking process* (Doctoral dissertation). Harvard Graduate School of Education, p. 45.

Radd, S., Generett, G. G., Gooden, M. A., & Theoharis, G. (2021). *Five practices for equity-focused school leadership.* ASCD.

Safir, S., & Dugan, J. (2021). *Street data: A next generation model for equity, pedagogy, and school transformation.* Corwin.

Singleton, G. E. (2015). *Courageous conversations about race* (2nd ed.). Corwin Press.

Tajfel, H., & Turner, J. C. (1979). An integrative theory of intergroup conflict. In W. G. Austin & S. Worchel (Eds.), *The social psychology of intergroup relations* (pp. 33–47). Brooks/Cole.

Torres, K., Lee, N., & Tran, C. (2015). *Building relationships: Bridging cultures—Cultural brokering in family engagement.* The Equitable Parent-School Collaboration Research Project. University of Washington School of Education.

University of Michigan. (2021). *Social identity wheel.* https://sites.lsa.umich.edu/inclusive-teaching/social-identity-wheel/

Zakszeski, B., Rutherford, L., Heidelburg, K., & Thomas, L. (2021). In pursuit of equity: Discipline disproportionality and SWPBIS implementation in urban schools. *School Psychology, 36*(2), 122–130. https://doi.org/10.1037/spq0000428

Sample: Gonzala Elementary School: Embedding Equity, Inclusion, and Belonging in PBIS-Professional Learning Plan

	August	September	October	November	December
MTSS/PBIS Core Team	Evaluate disaggregated ODR data from previous year	Establish meeting agreements *Equity & PBIS Introductory Session: What is disproportionality?*	*Self-Awareness: What are social identities?*	*Self-Awareness: Vulnerable Decision Points*	Evaluate mid-year risk ratio data in ODR data—Seek out possible VDPs impacting the system
MTSS/PBIS Advanced Tier Team	Evaluate the progress of students in advanced tiers from end of previous year	Establish meeting agreements *Equity & PBIS Introductory Session: What is disproportionality?*	*Self-Awareness: What are social identities?*	*Self-Awareness: Vulnerable Decision Points*	Analyze advanced tiered supports and seek out any potential VDPs impacting student performance

(Continued)

(*Continued*)

	August	September	October	November	December
Grade-Level Teams	Review prior year data for incoming students (academics, SEL, behavior)	MTSS Team representatives highlight identified outcome goals for the quarter with grade-level teams	*Equity & PBIS Introductory Session: What is disproportionality?*		*Self-Awareness: What are social identities?* Facilitated by core team representatives and core team coach
Full Faculty	*What is Equity, Inclusion & Belonging 101?*				Completion of staff climate survey (assessing belonging, safety)

	January	February	March	April	May
MTSS/ PBIS Core Team	*What are Neutralizing Routines?* Professional Learning Session	Engage with cultural brokers via families or communities to enhance team responsiveness	Using feedback and team membership of cultural brokers, review current matrices, agreements, expectations, etc.	Update and showcase new matrices, agreements and expectations for team review and approval	Evaluate end-of-year risk ratio data in ODR data—Seek out possible VDPs impacting the system
MTSS/ PBIS Advanced Tier Team	*What are Neutralizing Routines?* Professional Learning Session	Engage with cultural brokers via families or communities to enhance team responsiveness	Using feedback and team membership of cultural brokers, review current intervention menu to ensure cultural responsivity	Update and showcase an intervention menu for team review and approval	Analyze advanced tiered supports and seek out any potential VDPs impacting student performance

(Continued)

(*Continued*)

	January	February	March	April	May
Grade-Level Teams	MTSS team representatives and coach review mid-year data with teams and discuss any identified disproportionality	*What are Neutralizing Routines?* Professional Learning Session	MTSS team representatives and coach engage teams in identifying VDPs and develop individual neutralizing routines	MTSS team representatives and coach engage teams in reviewing individual neutralizing routines and creating team-based routines	MTSS team representatives and coach engage in a review of team routines. What's working? What should change?
Full Faculty	Review results of climate survey with faculty—Create subcommittees among staff for specific feedback on strategies to enhance climate	Office hours with members of the core or advanced tiers team to have a thought-partner or pose questions on equity, inclusion, and belonging through issues related to discipline, academics, or social-emotional learning—Ongoing work from subcommittees on ways to maintain a positive school climate			*Look Back Session* What worked? What should change? Are we meeting our mission/vision?

Checklist for Equitable Acknowledgment Systems for Students

Key Questions:

Per grade level/department, how many acknowledgments have been distributed across the month?

	August	Sept.	Oct.	Nov.	Dec.	Jan.	Feb.	Mar.	Apr.	May	June
1st grade											
2nd grade											
3rd grade											

Among the grade levels/departments, which students or student groups are not receiving the same level of acknowledgments? Can we hypothesize why not?

How do we know the acknowledgments are appropriate? Are students reporting positive experiences? Have we checked in with families as well?

Do we need to adjust any part of the acknowledgment system to provide access to more students (across the grade levels and based on our tier 1 data, where could we be more strategic)?

- ◆ **Acknowledgment Selection**
  - – Core team recommended
  - – Student/Family recommended
  - – Staff recommended
  - – Other input provided by: _____
- ◆ **Acknowledgment Criteria**
  - – May be offered in a variety of forms (e.g., tangible, participatory, etc.)
  - – Available to every student
  - – May not be removed once earned
  - – Is tied to student demonstrating agreed upon school-wide expectations (e.g., 3Rs)

Checklist for Equitable Acknowledgment Systems for Staff

Key Questions:

Per grade level/department, how many acknowledgments have been distributed across the month for staff?

	Aug.	Sept.	Oct.	Nov.	Dec.	Jan.	Feb.	Mar.	Apr.	May	June
1st grade team											
2nd grade team											
Custodial Staff											

Among the grade levels/departments, which staff are not receiving the same level of acknowledgments? Can we hypothesize why not?

How are our staff acknowledgments being received? Have we checked in with the staff to see if we could do something different?

- ◆ **Acknowledgment Selection**
  - – Core team recommended
  - – Student/Family recommended
  - – Staff recommended
  - – Other input provided by: _____
- ◆ **Acknowledgment Criteria**
  - – May be offered in a variety of forms (e.g., tangible, participatory, etc.)
  - – Available to every staff member (e.g., custodial staff, secretary, counselors, etc.)
  - – May not be removed once earned
  - – Is tied to staff demonstrating agreed upon school-wide expectations (e.g., 3Rs)

5

Where Do We Go From Here?

What's Next?

As a reader of this text, you may be asking yourself, "What should our PBIS team address first?" Or you may be questioning if this is all too much to tackle at once. Your concerns and reservations are valid. The work of embedding equitable processes into implementation of PBIS or any other innovation requires time and stamina. Systems change often takes between 3 to 5 years to see any measurable shift (Fixsen et al., 2007). School-based teams would be wise to action plan using long-term objectives to ensure the implementation and sustainability process is sound.

Intentionality in the work of equity, inclusion, and belonging is pivotal for sustainable outcomes. The HELP framework, created by Dr. Ronald W. Whitaker, II (Misner, 2021), offers a way to understand and implement equitable practices in education. Table 5.1 highlights the components of the HELP framework. As described, simply engaging in equitable practices without foundational understanding of the history of oppressive systems, the difference between equality and equity, and without a focus on authentic relationships will often result in implementation drift, helplessness, or moving on to the next best thing.

DOI: 10.4324/9781003294351-5

Table 5.1 The Critical HELP Framework adapted from Dr. Ronald W. Whitaker, II (Misner, 2021)

HELP Framework	
History	Understanding the history of systemic barriers for marginalized and minoritized people and how it impacts disproportionate outcomes in education and other systemic structures (health, economics, housing).
Equality v. Equity	Understanding the importance of ensuring access and opportunities are distributed based on strengths and needs versus a one-size-fits-all approach.
Love	Authentic relationships among students, staff, families, and communities. Focusing on the value of human dignity.
Pedagogy & Practices	Applying culturally responsive, sustaining, and responsible practices, with the key tenets of history, equality versus equity, and love at the core.

This is a useful frame to consider as an overlay to the implementation science described throughout this text as a way to sustain a positive school climate. So often, in education, there is a push toward efficiency and completion. The need to *check boxes* may override the quality of supports or infrastructure. When data are pointing toward the need for systemic change, either through disproportionate outcomes in academics, social-emotional competencies, or behavior, focusing only at the student level will not create impactful change for the generations of students to come.

Throughout the previous chapters, foundational understanding has been established to anchor PBIS teams in their specific mission and vision for implementation with an equity mindset. Teaming structures have also been described in detail to support the importance of interdisciplinary perspectives. These structures serve as the foundation of sustaining equitable systems, data, and practices. As part of the PBIS team, the consistent assessment of the current system remains critical. Having the ability to determine through either audits, surveys, or anecdotal reports how the system is responding to all students and staff provides the guideposts for moving forward along the journey. These assessments offer teams the information to determine practices they should start, stop, or continue.

As the journey proceeds, data practices remain a cornerstone of the team process. Detecting disproportionality in discipline and access to mental health services and acknowledgment systems provides a *health check* of tiered support systems. As these practices become more fluent for teams, equity becomes a mindset and not simply an extra task. Data practices are not simply *crunching numbers* but being able to fully evaluate and interpret the provided information. Perception data, for instance, shares a story from the perspectives of multiple vested partners (e.g., families, staff, community, students). Their perceptions and input are the drivers of policies and practices. Their input helps teams determine if the actions taken are impactful or simply continuing a cycle of failure.

The chapters describing action planning and implementation are pivotal to ensuring the mission and vision of the school team are executed with fidelity. It provides teams with the *how* to create conditions for equitable access and opportunity. Although the focus of the book was primarily situated in PBIS, the integration of academics and social-emotional competencies are equally important in the process of providing a sense of belonging for all students. The educational experience when academics, behavior, and social-emotional wellness are adequately addressed allows for students to be viewed through a multidimensional lens.

Where do we go from here? How do we ensure we are meeting the needs of every learner through the PBIS framework? What if everyone is not in agreement with how we have adjusted our implementation? These are pivotal questions as you have digested the contents of this text thus far. PBIS as a framework is rooted in creating and sustaining positive school climates. Unfortunately, in some cases, implementation of the framework has created settings where specific student groups are still unable to fully experience the benefit of a positive climate and are still unable to feel a sense of connection to their school community. This chapter seeks to reimagine traditional PBIS into a framework that is truly accessible to every learner and community. The core components of systems, data, practices, and outcomes are only solid when equity is at the center. With that foundation in mind, there is the ability to provide culturally responsive and responsible implementation.

Culturally Responsive PBIS

How can PBIS teams create the conditions for each of these core components to become operationalized? Sure, it seems easy when we read various strategies and ideas, but what does PBIS look like, sound like, and feel like when it is responsive to the cultures represented in a school or district? Culture is not exclusive to race and ethnicity and includes religion, socioeconomic status, gender identity, sexual orientation, disability status, home language(s), family background, etc. As described by the vignettes offered in previous chapters, culturally responsive approaches in PBIS are needed in rural, suburban, and urban settings. It is not a specific type of PBIS that would only be applicable in a specific place or with a specific group of students or communities. It is recommended that from the foundation of either exploring PBIS or initial installation, embedding culturally responsive practices is a necessary first step to ensure effective implementation (Heidelburg et al., 2022).

The Center on PBIS (www.pbis.org) has a host of resources related to equity in the PBIS framework and offers the following core components for a culturally responsive PBIS framework: (1) Identity, (2) Voice, (3) Supportive Environment, (4) Situational Appropriateness, and (5) Data for Equity (Leverson et al., 2021). Each of these core components are valuable for PBIS teams as they consider their initial year of planning for installation of PBIS. As noted in Chapter 2, an audit or inventory of the current tools, processes, policies, and climate are necessary to begin the process of determining the multiple cultures that may exist in your school. These cultures may include those of students and families and should most certainly include staff. Understanding schools as microcosms of society and embedding culturally responsive practices into the PBIS framework would not be a simple add-on to the existing method of installation. Leverson et al., (2021) described the multiple identities to consider when developing systemic practices, including student identities, staff identities, community identity, and school identity. Developing a building-wide matrix, building an acknowledge system, and creating a discipline flow chart are valuable components of the PBIS framework. Developing these through the lens of one group/identity would not allow for all those who comprise the system to have the opportunity to successfully access the framework and create sustainable outcomes.

Often this is seen during an initial year of implementation, when the focus of the team may be on acknowledgments and event planning. Without the data analysis, action planning, and recognizing that certain students are not experiencing school climate in the same way, teams may falsely assume that *PBIS does not work* or *PBIS does not work for a school like ours*. This may also occur when the installation of PBIS is tied to funding. Often the funding will supply the *rewards* for the acknowledgment system and once those funds are no longer available, teams will abandon implementation as it is viewed as *too expensive* to maintain. While these are roadblocks to sustainability, these roadblocks are exacerbated in settings where there is a missing approach of embedding culturally relevant and responsible practices.

One of the authors served as an internal coach for PBIS at a small urban middle school. The school was not considered a place for positive school climate. Staff morale was low, fights were frequent among students, and the perception from the community was that the building was not safe. When PBIS was introduced to the faculty, following the core team engaging in the training and planning year, there was anxiety in how the information would be received. In particular, there was concern around staff members who had taught in the building for a long time and those with referent power among the staff. Essentially, if these staff members did not agree or support the new initiative it was highly unlikely the staff would buy-in and give their best effort. As the core team presented the overview of PBIS, there were immediate questions around rewarding behaviors students in middle school should already know how to exhibit. One staff member, in particular, said she had read all about this and this was just another attempt to bring something new into the district that never worked in schools like this. She repeated that our students were *different* and what worked in the suburbs would never work here. Many of the staff nodded in agreement, and it was clear that this would be a difficult journey. The core team knew that it had some important discussions ahead and yet were more determined than ever to give it their best try.

Initially, the core team was struggling to remain positive about the year ahead but were coordinated in their next approach with the faculty. At the next professional development day, they asked each grade level to meet as a team and develop lesson plans based on the expectations of Be Ready, Be Responsible, Be Respectful for locations in the building, including classrooms. The team noticed staff were more engaged in this process and decided the next step when engaging with faculty would be to introduce a draft flowchart for consequences. The flowchart would designate what behaviors were considered classroom-managed and administrator-managed. The staff expressed how they felt heard in the discussion around the flowchart and appreciated that it was not just developed and then pushed out to them. One of the modifications to the originally developed flowchart included the addition of counselor-managed behaviors in an effort to interrupt the need for an immediate referral to the office. As the team processed through the installation phase of implementation, they centered the staff in as many decisions as possible. Eventually, those staff members who were resistant at first were beginning to show signs of connectedness, and the team felt like they had crossed a major hurdle.

Eventually, after 2 years of implementation, the funding that supplied the acknowledgment system for the building was no longer available. The team noticed a lack of implementation fidelity and that the referrals to the office were beginning to increase. The original staff members who expressed concern about adopting PBIS were back in their original mindset and were beginning to tell other staff members to just wait for the *next big thing*. At a team meeting, the school psychologist asked if the core team checked in with the students and families about how they were experiencing PBIS. The school psychologist recently attended a professional development session on family and community engagement and thought the team was lacking family input for their action plans. The team invited several family members to join the PBIS team; however, since the meetings were always held at 7:30 am, those family members often missed meetings or asked to be removed due to scheduling conflicts. It became clear that the focus of the buy-in was so heavily invested in staff, the team neglected to offer similar opportunities to students and families. That missing component was hindering the progress of their implementation efforts and appeared to impact the utility of the acknowledgment system and the buy-in from students and families around the expectations, and it seemed to contribute to dwindling momentum overall.

Without considering the importance of affirming identity, the voice and agency of the families, communities, and, ultimately, students a void is created in connecting the practices to long-term outcomes. Voice and agency are more than offering students the opportunity to speak at meetings or complete surveys. While these are important, if those voices are not diverse or are only considered for the purposes of compliance, the absence of authentic input necessary for improvement will continue to perpetuate the same cycles of status quo. Some may say we have students from all different types of groups, and we ensure there is no overrepresentation of one voice over others. This is great practice, and yet there still may be some voices that may be in the margins, who either do not feel comfortable expressing themselves for fear of retaliation, those who are neurodivergent, or who have not been offered other methods of providing input.

As teams continue to leverage and honor the voices of those they serve, the development of policies and practices is a step in creating an environment where authentic connections to the school as a place of safety are made. PBIS embedded with culturally responsive practices would have the following characteristics:

◆ Clear channels of communication between students, staff, and community for continued cycles of improvement.
◆ A review of data (office discipline referrals, acknowledgment delivery system, survey/perceptions) with an equity mindset.
 – Monthly review of office discipline referral data at tier 1
 – Quarterly review of risk indices and risk ratios
 – Review of survey/perception data completed by students,

staff, or families more than once per year; these surveys may be given to different groups at various times throughout the year

◆ A consistent review and adjustment (if needed) of acknowledgment systems to determine their utility and access for every student.

◆ A consistent review and adjustment (if needed) of the discipline/consequence system to determine if specific processes are impacting specific student groups disproportionately.

Tier 1 implementation is also relevant to specific classroom practices. Throughout the authors' experiences in consultation, it is almost certain the highest amount of office discipline referrals are from the classroom (Gion, et al., n.d.). Engaging instructional practices offer a way to create culturally responsive classroom experiences for every student. Chapparo and colleagues (2015) described four practices to increase equity through instruction. These included: (1) use of explicit instruction, (2) building and priming background knowledge, (3) increased opportunities to respond, and (4) providing performance feedback. Each of these culturally responsive practices allow the instructor to provide a climate of learning where voices are valued and differences are honored. Zaretta Hammond (2015) described the importance of culturally responsive teaching and defines it as follows:

> An educator's ability to recognize students' cultural displays of learning and meaning making and respond positively and constructively with teaching moves that use cultural knowledge as a scaffold to connect what the student knows to new concepts and content in order to promote effective information processing. All the while, the educator understands the importance of being in a relationship and having a social-emotional connection to the student in order to create a safe space for learning.
>
> (p. 15)

The integration of culturally responsive practices for academics, social-emotional wellness, and behavior is a necessary component of shared ownership in a tiered system of support.

While much of the focus on creating an equitable PBIS is on tier 1, the advanced tiers also require embedded culturally responsive practices. Each system will have a different contextual fit with regard to the types of interventions needed. Regardless, the interventions selected and delivered through the system of support will need to be provided with intentionality. This may be reflected in the access students have to tier 2 supports without a rush to move to tier 3 supports due to perceived lack of progress. Each intervention or layered support onto tier 1 should be based on the data obtained as the student progresses and appropriate based upon student needs.

As the interventions become more individualized at the tier 3 level, the intentional inclusion of the family and any community-based supports would be necessary. However, simply inviting these partners to meetings would not be enough to provide them the opportunity to offer their expertise in how to support the student. A family-school partnership is defined as "a child-focused approach wherein families and professionals cooperate, coordinate, and collaborate to enhance opportunities and success for children and adolescents across social, emotional, behavioral, and academic domains" (Sheridan et al., 2014, p. 440). This type of family-school partnership is more intensive than the inclusion of families in shaping the infrastructure of the system at tier 1. This engagement requires seeing the families or community supports as an equal partner and influential in accountability and goal-setting around the student's progress.

Culturally responsive PBIS is the goal of effective PBIS. At the initial development of PBIS as a framework, there was neither a specific focus on the cultural backgrounds of students and how that informs staff responses to their behaviors nor was it designed to mitigate disciplinary disparities (Heidelburg et al., 2022). Over time, and through research (McIntosh et. al., 2018; Vincent et al., 2015), the need to leverage PBIS as a vehicle to reduce disproportionate outcomes for every student has become an imperative to change the trajectories for learners in multiple domains (academic, behavioral, social-emotional). For example, Payno-Simmons (2021) described a pilot in Michigan where specific processes embedding equitable approaches as part of PBIS implementation were provided over 3 years. Using core components such as consistent use of disaggregated data, implementing a culturally responsive framework, and teaching the use of neutralizing routines to mitigate implicit bias, the pilot site was able to see a gap reduction between Black and White students in their risk ratios over time. Additionally, there was greater awareness among staff in recognizing their own deficit thinking or biased decision making. These processes and strategies are not simple or quickly installed. However, this study demonstrated the importance of tenacity and long-term commitment to a necessary change. This is one example of the importance of embedding culturally responsive PBIS as part of the implementation process. Imagine your school and using these strategies to see more positive outcomes for students with disabilities, students who receive free and reduced lunch, students of varying gender identities, and students who have experienced trauma, among others. There are great possibilities!

The previous chapters have highlighted the core constructs teams should consider as they build and sustain a positive school climate through an equitable PBIS system. Reflecting upon the HELP framework (Misner, 2021), culturally responsive PBIS provides the vehicle for an understanding of history, the difference between providing equal versus equitable practices, engaging in authentic relationships, and implementing pedagogy and practices that are engaging, responsive, and relevant for students.

How Do We Address Pushback?

Change in any system is rarely met with immediate buy-in. A new concept, process, or innovation has to be introduced in a way that allows individuals to understand the purpose, goal, and potential benefits of implementation. When considering systems change for large-scale shifts in positive climate, culture, and equity, there is always the potential for those who are content in the current structure to question the need for change. Others who have heard about similar changes may be hesitant based on their interpretation of how it worked or did not work for others. Still, some others will resist simply due to fear or concern that they will lose something in the process. Loss can resemble many things, such as loss of services, loss of materials, loss of privileges, loss of power, etc. When these perceived losses are associated with a new innovation or system change, resistance increases.

The authors of this text have encountered consultation with school-based teams that are either experiencing initiative fatigue, fear disrupting the status quo, or simply see the change as too dramatic or challenging in their setting. In each of these instances, unfortunately, progress toward improving sustainable outcomes has suffered. In many cases it was considering a new way of approaching universal screening or it was abandoning curriculum or programs that were not leading to an effective response to intervention model. In other instances, it was seeking to revise and reconfigure a discipline code of conduct or embed social-emotional instruction provided by the teacher in each classroom. The information provided throughout this text described strategies and recommendations that may cause pushback or resistance. Discussing topics such as culture, equity, race, gender, religion, access, etc. are not easy discussions. They are especially more difficult in school settings where there are so many different opinions, perceptions, and beliefs regarding the appropriateness of having these discussions at all. This is the importance of remaining committed to your respective school's or district's mission and vision. In many cases, districts have adopted mission statements that speak directly to providing positive learning environments for every student. They may also describe producing excellence in education. Each of these examples are directly connected to equitable and positive school climates. A place where students, staff, families, and communities from all walks of life have the opportunity to experience an educational system made especially for them to succeed in society.

Consider the vignette from Chapter 4 at Gonzala Elementary School, and their principal Mrs. Book. As a recap, Mrs. Book attended a professional development session on disproportionality in discipline and asked her district PBIS coach to analyze the building discipline data and particularly risk ratios. The data showed the following risk ratio results:

Black/African American–2.7
White–1.2
Asian–0.5
Hispanic/Latino/a/x–1.7
Multi-Racial–2.0

After reviewing the data, Mrs. Book called her team together to problem-solve how to reduce these disproportionate outcomes. Mrs. Book was especially concerned about the data for Black/African American and Multi-Racial students. The team was mixed in their reactions to the data. Some offered that the students who identified as Black/African American or Multi-Racial typically came from homes where education was not valued, and their behaviors reflected what their parents tolerated. Others seemed genuinely dismayed by the data and wondered how these numbers were accurate and what they could do differently.

Mrs. Book had a hypothesis that the top reason for referral for students who identified as Black/African American and Multi-Racial was for disrespect. She had learned that this was a highly subjective behavior and would be potentially influenced by implicit bias. Mrs. Book consulted with her district PBIS coach to determine an appropriate professional learning sequence for her team and apply those skills in their upcoming meetings and data analysis.

Mrs. Book asked the school psychologist, school counselor, and district PBIS coach to present at the following faculty meeting and display the current data for their discipline referrals. She asked for the initial data set to be an aggregate of their overall referrals and indicating time, location, perceived functions of behavior, problem behaviors, and grade levels. She wanted the faculty to see the types of information the core PBIS team reviewed on a monthly basis and obtain the faculty's initial reactions to their view of the data. In small groups, she asked other core team members to facilitate conversations about the data and gather ideas from faculty on different approaches to reduce problem behaviors based on their review. This portion of the meeting went well, and staff were engaged in the process.

For the second half of the meeting, Mrs. Book asked the district coach to display the disaggregated data and explain the concepts of risk ratios. She anticipated similar reactions to what she experienced when the data was initially provided to the core team; however she was gobsmacked when some staff instantly left the meeting and indicated that they were not racists and were offended that they were being treated as though they were targeting certain students. Others became emotional and said they were doing their best and what more did she want from them. Others sat in awe of what they were witnessing. Mrs. Book also noticed a few of her staff of color who seemed emotionless and some with looks of disgust.

The entire episode impacted the core PBIS team and how they moved forward. Mrs. Book knew that she needed to debrief with the team and that somehow she missed the mark for what she intended to highlight during the meeting. She had hoped to use the data display as an introduction to the staff of the upcoming professional learning series she developed in collaboration with the district PBIS coach and thought it would be a way to connect the staff to the purpose of the learning. She also realized that her school psychologist, school counselor, and district PBIS coach were probably feeling the brunt of the pushback following the meeting, as they were the primary facilitators.

It seemed that before she could gather her thoughts and think about how to proceed with the core team, she received a phone call from the superintendent that there were several staff members who lodged formal complaints with his office. Additionally, some threatened to contact the local media, and some already contacted parents who felt Mrs. Book was creating a setting too focused on race. Other staff members contacted local community groups who applauded Mrs. Book *exposing* the data and wanted to know if that data could be made more public. She was in a very difficult position and throughout this time knew that her goal was to make her school more inclusive, welcoming, and accessible to every learner.

The next core team meeting began by Mrs. Book opening the space for teammates to authentically share their viewpoints on the meeting, beginning with what went well and how they would have approached things differently. Some team members felt empowered to move forward now that the data was out there showing everyone that there was an opportunity to do better work. Others were fearful for their positions and the relationships they had established with staff who were offended by the way the data was presented. Others said they felt numb and sadly expected the swift reactions. Holding this space was important to Mrs. Book and helped her understand some of her own emotions and reactions. Once the team seemed ready to discuss how to move forward, Mrs. Book apologized to the team and said that she recognized her intentions were not fully fleshed out, and she inadvertently placed her teammates in tough positions.

The team offered that they needed to consider how to restore trust among the staff and also not allow themselves to be deterred from making changes that would ultimately benefit students who were not accessing the PBIS framework in the same way as their peers. They all agreed that if they could remain focused on that imperative focus, they would need to withstand the pushback and continue to listen and learn from their colleagues, families, and students. The superintendent asked to attend the team meeting and offered that when he faces pushback around his goals for the district, he often refers to the district's mission and vision as a way to anchor his ideas and ask if what he is considering honors the mission. Mrs. Book thought that would be a great way to restore trust among the staff while remaining authentic in the team's purpose for creating positive school climate. She also thought it would be important to create focus groups to hear from the community and the families to help them also understand the reason for evaluating and disaggregating the data. Although there are no easy solutions in these situations, there are steps forward to support a school's ultimate goal of producing global citizens.

Transparency, plain language, and a commitment to the mission are three of the most important pieces of addressing pushback. Transparency may look like holding community and family listening sessions where the team holds a session to discuss the new innovation or framework being adopted. It allows families and other partners to gain an understanding, pose questions, and express their concerns. Pushback related to equitable PBIS may be rooted in misinformation or rooted in strong belief systems. Belief systems may be very difficult to shift.

However, if pushback is a result of misinformation, the ability to educate partners, while using plain language as a strategy, often leads to more productive dialogue. Pushback is hard, and it can sometimes deter well-intended teams from moving forward. Be encouraged. While pushback is expected it should not influence progress when the goal is to create a more positive climate for every student. We can all agree that a student should be able to experience school in a way that allows them to thrive.

Conclusion

This text has offered effective practices when considering systems-level change, regardless of the innovation. Ultimately, the goal of the text has been to provide guidance on enhancing the infrastructure of educational systems. No longer can we simply remain content with groups of students lacking opportunity and access to positive and inclusive learning environments. As systems-level thinkers in education, school-based teams are primed to set conditions for every student and staff to engage in a healthy and safe experience. As you, the reader, evaluate your current implementation status, discipline, access to advanced placement courses, enrichment opportunities, perception data, short-term and long-term goals consider the foundation of your tiered system.

Ask the following:

- Is our foundation solid? How do we know?
- Is our foundation shaky? What can we fix immediately?
- Who have we neglected?
- Which voices are not heard?
- What are the small wins?
- How will we know we have made a shift?

These answers will inform how you build the rest of the infrastructure of tiered supports. At tier 1, universal practices will be indicative of the health of the system and provide information on how to best construct the allocation of resources for the advanced tiers. Without these important checkpoints, the implementation process may stall and/or evaporate. As you embark on the journey to create an equitable PBIS framework in your respective system, remember that this work is hard, you will experience challenges, and there may be times when you will want to abandon the work. It is imperative to focus on the long-term effects of impacting a student who has never before had a sense of belonging in school. Their story could change dramatically, simply validating the importance of their educational experience by seeking to make it better.

We hope you have enjoyed your journey thus far, and we hope you have been inspired to go forth and make change that is meaningful.

Chapter 5: Seeds for Growth

- ◆ The work of embedding equitable processes into implementation of PBIS or any other innovation requires **time** and **stamina**.
- ◆ When data are pointing toward the **need for systemic change**, either through disproportionate outcomes in academics, social-emotional competencies, or behavior, focusing *only* at the **student level** will **not** create **impactful change** for the generations of students to come.
- ◆ It is recommended, that from the **foundation** of either exploring PBIS or initial installation, **embedding culturally responsive practices** is a necessary **first** step to ensure effective implementation (Heidelburg et al., 2022).
- ◆ Voice and agency is **more** than offering students the opportunity to speak at meetings or complete surveys. While these are important, if those voices are not diverse or are only considered for the purposes of compliance, the **authentic input** necessary for improvement will continue to perpetuate the same cycles of status quo.
- ◆ **Transparency**, **plain language**, and a **commitment** to the mission are three of the most important pieces of addressing pushback.

Table 5.2 Demographic characteristics of McDowell Middle School

Characteristic	Proportion of Student Population
Asian	3.3%
Black/African American	1.5%
Hispanic/Latino/a/x	8.7%
White	81.4%
Multi-Racial	5.0%
Economically Disadvantaged	27.0%
English Learner	2.2%
Special Education	18.7%
Foster Care	0.1%
Homeless	0.8%

Vignette

In the following vignette, we will introduce you to the core PBIS team from McDowell Middle School (fictitious school name). The team consists of the following members: building principal, school counselor, school psychologist, sixth grade teacher leader, seventh grade teacher leader, eighth grade teacher leader, reading specialist, art teacher, and family liaison. McDowell Middle School has the following demographics as shown in Table 5.2.

This vignette will highlight the school counselor's (internal coach) journal of progress for the team. As you review her captured experiences of McDowell's journey toward creating an equitable PBIS, consider the following questions: (1) Can you see yourself or your team in any of the journal entries? (2) Which areas resonate? (3) What interests you as something new you would try along your journey? and (4) What would you do differently to fit your context?

September 2023
We are simply devastated. Our behaviors are out of control and the school year has just begun. We keep hearing about PBIS and how it

could potentially help. We've never had this many referrals so early and the staff are experiencing burnout. I feel helpless and can't see how we will make it to December, let alone June. We need something, but I don't want to just pick up something that wastes our time or makes our staff even more upset. I've talked with our principal, and we are going to leverage our leadership team to begin thinking about what might work best for us.

January 2024

We have begun training around PBIS, and I have to be honest, I am skeptical. They are discussing rewards and I can already picture those staff who will not agree to that. Especially, at the middle school level, where students are expected to know how to appropriately behave. However, the team seems excited to try and are willing to talk to those staff, we anticipate may be resistant.

May 2024

We've started building out our plans for next year, and we have realized that we were missing core components in our system, like a consequence structure, an acknowledgment system, and a way to effectively review our disciplinary data. Who knew?! We are so excited to get started and to begin bringing our staff on board with this new framework. We've heard from families that they are disappointed in how our school has become unsafe, and we are so ready for change!

August 2024

Well . . . we held our first faculty meeting to introduce PBIS and asked the staff to help us create a matrix for expectations in various locations in the school building. It went surprisingly well! Interestingly, our family liaison noted that she's been speaking with some of our families, who identify as Latino/a/x, and they are interested in helping us better understand how to better partner with them. We've decided to have our team meet with representatives from our families who'd like to support this effort.

September 2024

We just installed a new system that allows us to look at our office discipline referrals and it's so helpful! We can see at our monthly meetings where, what, who, when, days of the week and potential functions of the behaviors we are noticing in the submitted referrals. We've partnered with an external coach from our district level PBIS team who is helping us understand and analyze the data. This process has been a real game-changer for many of our teammates. I'm noticing some who are personalizing the data or attempting to blame specific students for the high number of referrals from certain grade levels. I have my work cut out, but our external coach shared that this is normal at first, and we need to develop some agreements for how we discuss the data.

May 2024

This year has been eye-opening, we've built a pretty solid structure around PBIS at McDowell. We still have some naysayers, but overall, the students and staff seem happy with the acknowledgments and have an understanding that we're using data to make decisions. Our principal looks way more relaxed too! However, I just attended a national conference and I learned about disproportionality, and I am concerned we are not being equitable in how our referrals are being delivered, or even our acknowledgments, yikes!

August 2024

My principal encouraged me to collaborate with the school psychologist in seeing how we might be able to calculate risk indices and risk ratios. We reviewed last year's data and unfortunately, when we did the calculations, our multi-racial students were overrepresented in the data for disrespect and defiance. We saw similar overrepresentation for our students identified with an IEP. Where have we gone wrong?! How did we miss this? I learned about subjectivity and how that leads to referring too many students who may not match the staff member's individual perspective. I am interested in finding a tool to evaluate our system and progress to help us know if we're being culturally responsive. That data may help me make the case for more intentional professional learning for our team and for our staff. I have a call in to my principal and our external coach tomorrow. We've got to do something!

September 2024

We held our first professional learning session with our core team around disproportionality in discipline. As part of the session, I was asked to help the team recall our risk ratio information and how subjective behaviors may be impacting the number of referrals we are receiving. I asked the team to do some pre-work and visit the Center on PBIS website and review their Equity page. In particular, anything they could find on vulnerable decision points and neutralizing routines. Many expressed that they were intrigued by those concepts but unsure if they would be able to recognize the VDPs that may be related to implicit bias. Hunger and fatigue made sense but bias seemed far-fetched for some of them. I was thankful for this dialogue because at least they were open to learning more and I was more than happy to continue to build on their curiosity. Admittedly, while I feel confident in continuing the learning, I think it may be time to ask for some support to co-facilitate these upcoming sessions, where we begin to take a deeper look at our own self-awareness. I am not ashamed to name that I still have my own learning to do and want to be the best support I can as we implement this important work. I just have to keep remembering that we are experiencing discomfort in order to create action that ultimately helps students in the end.

Reference List

Chaparro, E., Nese, R. N. T., & McIntosh, K. (2015). *Examples of engaging instruction to increase equity in education.* Center on PBIS. www.pbis.org.

Fixsen, D., Naoom, S., Blasé, K., & Wallace, F. (2007). Implementation: The missing link between research and practice. *American Professional Society on the Abuse of Children (APSAC) Advisor,* 19(1–2), 4–12.

Gion, C. M., McIntosh, K., & Horner, R. (n.d.). *Patterns of minor office discipline referrals in schools using SWIS*. https://assets-global. website-files.com/5d3725188825e071f1670246/5d7979befedbb 681be830b04_final-odr-brief.pdf

Hammond, Z. (2015). *Culturally responsive teaching and the brain*. Corwin.

Heidelburg, K., Rutherford, L., & Parks, T. W. (2022). A preliminary analysis assessing SWPBIS implementation fidelity in relation to disciplinary outcomes of black students in urban schools. *The Urban Review*, 54(3), 138–154. https://doi.org/10.1007/s11256-021-00609

Leverson, M., Smith, K., McIntosh, K., Rose, J., & Pinkelman, S. (2021, March). *PBIS cultural responsiveness field guide: Resources for trainers and coaches*. Center on PBIS. www.pbis.org

McIntosh, K., Gion, C., & Bastable, E. (2018). *Do schools implementing SWPBIS have decreased racial and ethnic disproportionality in school discipline?* Center on PBIS. www.pbis.org

Misner, S. (2021, January 15). The critical HELP framework by Dr. Ronald W. Whitaker, II. *MCIU Learning Network*. https://learn.mciu. org/the-critical-help-framework-by-dr-ronald-w-whitaker-ii/

Payno-Simmons, R. L. (2021). Centering equity in school discipline: The Michigan PBIS equity pilot. *Preventing School Failure: Alternative Education for Children and Youth*, 65(4), 343–353. doi:10.1080/10 45988X.2021.1937024

Sheridan, S. M., Clarke, B. L., & Christenson, S. L. (2014). Best practices in promoting family engagement in education. In P. L. Harrison & A. Thomas (Eds.), *Best practices in school psychology: Systems-level services* (pp. 439–454). National Association of School Psychologists.

Vincent, C. G., Sprague, J. R., Pavel, M., Tobin, T., & Gau, J. (2015). Effectiveness of schoolwide positive behavior interventions and supports in reducing racially inequitable disciplinary exclusion. In D. J. Losen (Ed.), *Closing the school discipline gap: Equitable remedies for excessive exclusion* (pp. 208–221). Teachers College Press.

Creating Psychologically Safe Professional Learning Spaces

A key component of equitable PBIS implementation is to address system, data, and practices. Embedding equity, inclusion, and belonging into the implementation process is deeply rooted in continuous professional learning and growth. Developing psychologically safe professional learning spaces are important to ensure implementation is not thwarted or stalled.

Establish relational and operational agreements	• Teams are encouraged to create an atmosphere where participants are aware and able to understand the ways they will interact and determine action.
	• Relational agreements create the ways teammates interact with each other. This may include:
	  • Honoring diverse perspectives
	  • Listening without judgment
	  • Leading with curiosity
	• Operational agreements create the ways teammates consider and execute action. This may include:
	  • Determining roles for teammates (e.g., facilitator, timekeeper, etc.)
	  • Established check-in points on progress (e.g., weekly, monthly, quarterly)
	  • Positing questions to check for equitable access and opportunity

Take your time	• Recognize that the creation of psychologically safe professional learning spaces requires time, trust, and vulnerability. Allowing processes to be extended over multiple meetings, sessions, etc. is optimal. While matters may be urgent and need swift action, creating sustainable practices is time-intensive.

(Continued)

Share stories	• Trust-building is exercising relational agreements may come through teammates being able to describe their experiences and how they are engaging in the learning process. This opportunity may elicit discomfort but also may create more trust among the team for having authentic dialogue and see how their actions may have an impact on the students they are serving.
Embed action into the relational process	• To avoid spending too much time in relational processes, teams will need to consider how to balance the necessary time for establishing interactional functions with initial action items to translate their learning into practice. As PBIS implementers, teams may begin this by evaluating their own vulnerable decision points and creating neutralizing routines in their practice.

Quick Map of Equitable PBIS: Where Are We?

◆ Establish foundational understanding of equity, inclusion, and belonging
  – Have we unpacked how equity, inclusion, and belonging impact our system?
  – What is needed?
  – Who is impacted?
  – Do we have a sense of urgency?
◆ Beginning the journey
  – Exploration
  – Teaming
  – Audits
  – Data sources (e.g., academic, behavioral, social-emotional)

◆ Implementation and evaluation
  - Installation
  - Sustainability
  - Disaggregated data
  - Disproportionality detection (e.g., risk index, risk ratio)
◆ Becoming data rich and information rich
  - Numbers to sense (e.g., action planning)
  - Humanize the data (e.g., attaching experiences to the information)
  - Established relational and operational team agreements
  - Continued professional learning
◆ Equitable practices in action
  - Equity of voice across systems
  - Identity affirmation (students and adults)
  - Staff wellness and morale
  - Positive school climate
  - Improved educational outcomes

For Product Safety Concerns and Information please contact our EU representative GPSR@taylorandfrancis.com Taylor & Francis Verlag GmbH, Kaufingerstraße 24, 80331 München, Germany

Printed and bound by CPI Group (UK) Ltd, Croydon, CR0 4YY
08/06/2025
01896999-0020